Praise for the first edition of *Discover Your Scottish Ancestry*

'Packed with hints and ideas for all interested in Scottish family history. The book is an excellent guide for beginners with hints on how to get the best of information that relatives can supply, how to choose a computer program and where to find useful records. For the more experienced genealogist there are sections on records that may be found about specific occupations, or subjects. There is a good chapter on how to present your family history . . . This is one book that would be a useful addition to any family historian's bookshelf.'

Coontin Kin, Shetland Family History Society

'This book has a wealth of advice about traditional and non traditional sources . . . I liked the down-to-earth, simple explanations . . . you will also find a wealth of good topics to explore such as valuation rolls, poor law records, educational sources and occupational records among others. There is an excellent list of useful contact names and addresses.'

Glasgow & West of Scotland Family History Society newsletter

'This book is particularly welcome because many of the general guides to genealogy are written with English and Welsh family history in mind . . . Scotland is another country, with its own history, law and customs, with which researchers, to be successful, need to become familiar.'

Practical Family History

DISCOVER YOUR SCOTTISH ANCESTRY

Internet and Traditional Resources

Second edition

Graham S. Holton and Jack Winch

Edinburgh University Press

© Graham S. Holton and Jack Winch, 2009

First edition published 2003

Edinburgh University Press Ltd
22 George Square, Edinburgh
www.euppublishing.com

Reprinted 2010

Typeset in Minion Pro by
Servis Filmsetting Ltd, Stockport, Cheshire, and
printed and bound in Great Britain by
CPI Antony Rowe, Chippenham and Eastbourne

A CIP record for this book is available from the British Library

ISBN 978 0 7486 3920 5 (hardback)
ISBN 978 0 7486 3919 9 (paperback)

CONTENTS

FOREWORD

Over the years since the first publication of *Discover Your Scottish Ancestry*, interest in family history research has burgeoned, at least partly attributable to heightened media attention to the subject. As with our first edition, we aim to appeal both to beginners and to those who already have some experience of family history research. Although technology has had a major impact on family history, the traditional methods and principles of research still form the essential core of this fascinating subject. We hope that our advice will give you a good grounding in these methods and principles and that the bibliography and list of websites will allow you to investigate more fully any particular areas of interest.

Since the publication of the first edition, a continuous stream of major sources has become available on the Internet, resulting in a pressing need for this updated edition. We would emphasise the importance of ultimately basing family history research on original sources, which makes the trend to provide online access to images of primary sources a particularly significant one. Genetic testing, the other major development which we identified in 2003, is gradually becoming established as a tool to aid genealogical research. As a result, a complete chapter is devoted to the subject in this new edition. Further refinements can be expected over the coming years and perhaps even new tests may emerge which could increase the value of genetic testing to genealogists.

It is our continuing aim to provide a good grounding in the basics of Scottish family history research whilst also opening up avenues to further study for both the developing and the experienced family history researcher.

INTRODUCTION

'Why, oh why, do I want to research my family history?' Have you ever stopped to think?

You may have only a hazy idea of your motives, or you may have some very specific reason for embarking on this 'family history business'.

Maybe it is purely for the fun of it; of discovering your 'roots', delving into the unknown. Where were your ancestors born, where did they live, what were their occupations and what sort of lives did they lead? You may well, as many families do, have some family tradition that a particular relative was present at some historic event, or even left an unclaimed fortune. Such stories have perhaps spurred you into action, in an attempt to prove their truth or otherwise. Despite natural scepticism, there is very often a grain of truth in such traditions but at the same time they are not usually 'the whole truth'.

FAMILY TRADITIONS

Here is one amongst several stories in one of the authors' families, part of which has been proven by means of several sources. According to family legend a McArthur ancestor was a ship's surgeon aboard the *Victory* at the Battle of Trafalgar in 1805.

After some work, the author's descent from a Florence McArthur in Glasgow was traced and some time later, he discovered a substantial entry for her grandson, Dr John Dougall, in *Who's Who in Glasgow in 1909*. There was, of course, plenty of interesting information about John Dougall himself, including a photograph. However, the entry mentioned his relative 'Sir' Duncan McArthur, repeating the story that he had been aboard HMS *Victory* at Trafalgar. Finally, a copy of an article about Duncan was discovered in Glasgow City Archives, showing that he had in fact served on board the *Victory*, but about ten years prior to the Battle of Trafalgar. Also, although not actually knighted, he was awarded the CB, one rank below that of knighthood. This Duncan was a brother of Florence and son of Duncan, a gardener in Glasgow.

Amongst the traditions in your family folklore there may be claims to a relationship to a historical figure or to the nobility, which again you will be keen to investigate further. We will return to descents from the nobility later on in the book.

TALES OF THE UNEXPECTED

In the course of your researches, you may uncover a totally unexpected relationship. This happened in the course of one of our own pieces of research, when, having located a great-great-grandmother's death certificate, her mother's maiden name was found to be Munnings. As an interesting example of the unreliability of some sources, the mother's Christian name was recorded as Elizabeth, whereas when the great-great-grandmother's baptism was traced, her mother turned out to be Sarah Green Munnings. Sarah was a sister of William Green Munnings, the grandfather of Sir Alfred Munnings, a famous painter, best known for his paintings of horses and a controversial president of the Royal Academy.

PRIVATE DETECTIVE WORK

Family history research involves a considerable amount of detective work, often described as being like piecing together a jigsaw, and this aspect can prove quite exciting. As family lines lead off in different directions you could find yourself researching the history of an area, an occupation or an industry with which your family was connected and as a result gain new historical knowledge and insights. History can be given an added relevance when you know of your family's involvement. It becomes more personalised and has an added interest.

PRACTICAL BENEFITS

Those of you with a more practical motive behind your interest may have found that for legal or religious reasons you are required to undertake some research into your family's past. Anyone claiming a hereditary title in the United Kingdom must provide genealogical proof to substantiate their claim. In some European countries, proof of nobility over a certain period of time ensured the right to tax exemptions and entry to the army or civil service at a minimum rank and in some societies it has been necessary to show a family's high status to qualify for office. Although such needs may appear to apply mainly to the upper classes, the ordinary individual may also encounter similar needs. If an individual dies without leaving a will and has no known relatives, members of the family would be required to prove their relationship if they wished to inherit. Again, in medieval England, unfree tenants could not bring a case to court since they had no legal standing, but if they could prove a relationship to freemen, the case could go ahead. As a result, English medieval records contain genealogies of ordinary people recorded for this purpose.

Members of the Church of Jesus Christ of Latter-day Saints, or Mormons, as they are usually known, have a religious motive behind their enthusiasm for genealogy. Mormons are required to trace as many as possible of their ancestors so that they can be baptised by proxy. They believe that only those baptised by a Mormon priest can achieve full salvation and that this can be done for dead relatives whom they believe would have become Mormons had they had the opportunity. As a result, the Mormon Church has undertaken a vast amount of work in microfilming and inputting genealogical data to computer files. This has been of great benefit to genealogists throughout the world and as you might expect, the Mormons now have an enormous storehouse of information, which is contained in a huge underground library near Salt Lake City, USA. Some of the direct benefits of the work of the Mormons to other researchers such as ourselves will be mentioned later in the book.

IMPORTANCE OF FAMILY HISTORY TO OTHER SUBJECTS

We would like to point out here that, although family history has an obvious interest for the reasons already mentioned, its importance reaches much further, into the fields of local, economic and social history and historical demography. If we take a magnifying glass to the whole expanse of history we see the local history of each area and then, with a stronger lens, the family history of those who make up each individual community. In focusing on the individuals within a community, family history can illuminate and bring new perspectives to a study of a particular locality. Whether of high or low status, the family about which we are gathering information played a role in local society which was probably similar to that played by other families of comparable status. You may have information on the type of life lived by a whole section of the community or perhaps facts about a particular occupation important in the area. These are the sort of details which a local historian will need in order to provide a representative picture of life in the locality concerned. Such information can also be drawn upon by economic and social historians working on a broader scale and in particular by those studying historical demography.

Notable in this field in England has been the Cambridge Group for the History of Population and Social Structure, in particular Peter Laslett, R. S. Schofield and E. A. Wrigley. Since the 1960s they have been studying records of specific English parishes and applying statistical methods in order to analyse the populations and thereby draw conclusions. They have studied literacy, by looking at the ability to sign marriage registers or other documents and social structure from census returns and other listings of inhabitants. The main procedures they have used, however, are aggregation and family reconstitution. Aggregation uses the total figures of baptisms, marriages and burials from parish registers and is a fairly quick means of analysing population trends. The types of information gained are: the growth or decline of population; baptism, marriage and burial rates; marital fertility rates; infant mortality rates; mobility of population and illegitimacy rates.

Family reconstitution, although a much slower method, allows a more detailed and accurate analysis. In this case, information is gathered from various sources about members of particular families in order to 'reconstitute' them. Calculations are then made to establish: age at marriage; age at burial; age at the end of marriage; length of marriage; age of mother at baptisms of children; interval between baptisms and number of children. This information tells us a lot about the sociology of the family at different times and in different places and used together with data on the weather and harvest yields, the impact of epidemics and so on, can greatly increase our knowledge of the social and economic history of England.

In the process of family reconstitution, the historical demographers are doing much the same as the family historian but for a large number of families in a parish. The conclusions which they draw can provide a context within which to place our own family. Was our family and its individual members unusual in the time and place in question or did they follow the normal pattern of family life? This is the sort of question that we would like to answer and the methods and work of historical demographers may help us to do that.

Apart from the work of D. F. Macdonald, *Scotland's shifting population, 1770–1850*, published in 1937, the population history of Scotland received little attention until the 1970s, which saw the publication of *Scottish population history from the 17th century to the 1930s*, edited by Michael Flinn (1977). Over the last few years there have been various research projects on the subject based at the Universities of Strathclyde, Aberdeen, Glasgow and Lancaster and conclusions based on this research have appeared in various publications.

One particularly useful tool which can be used for the study of historical demography is the 1881 British census on CD-ROM. As we will show later in the book, it is possible to search for names throughout Scotland, England and Wales. Searches on occupations, addresses, ages and places of birth can also be made on individual regions, the last of these allowing the study of population movements.

GENEALOGY IN THE PAST

Throughout the ages, genealogy has varied in importance, depending on place and period and for widely differing reasons. Genealogists in the ancient world often traced the origins of a family or race back to gods and heroes. Genealogy helped to provide an extra unity to societies which emphasised kinship and demonstrated the necessary status which could entitle a family to an office, title or ownership of land. For example, Julius Caesar claimed descent from the Goddess Venus, through the Trojan Aeneas, while the Greeks Hippocrates and Aristotle both believed they were descended from Asclepius, the God of medicine. The Bible contains many genealogies tracing descents from Adam and Eve and in both China and Japan in ancient times, family records were well maintained. Most Chinese families kept a Generation Book, usually updated about every thirty years, which recorded births, marriages and deaths along with other information about the families. The Japanese government set up an office in 761 to record clan genealogies and within a hundred years or so more than 1,100 clans had been registered.

Medieval times saw the production of Norse sagas, Bede's *Ecclesiastical History of the English People*, the *Anglo-Saxon Chronicle* and Geoffrey of Monmouth's *History of the Kings of Britain*, in all of which a great interest in genealogy is evident. Descents from gods and heroes are numerous, but in most cases quite fictitious. In Scotland, the sennachies of the Highland clans were the bards who maintained the genealogical traditions of the clans. Their function was of great importance, not only because they could relate the ancestry of the members of the clan, linking them together and in some cases with the clan chief, but also because this information determined the rights of families to hold land and has been compared to the title deed in the feudal system.

From the sixteenth century, many genealogies were drawn up to prove the right to a coat of arms and to provide merchant and professional families with a high social status which they saw as important. By the end of the nineteenth century the production of genealogies was becoming much more scientific and the fabulous concoctions of the medieval genealogists were rejected. This reaction perhaps tended to go too far and the study of genealogy had reached a happy medium before the advent of the Internet. This development has led to a tendency towards assumptions in constructing family trees.

FACTORS IN TRACING ANCESTRY

Sir Anthony Wagner, in *English genealogy* (1983), identifies four factors governing the tracing of ancestry: status, record, name and continuity.

The status of a family in general affects the extent to which it appears in the records. The status may be that of a noble family, of landowners, of holders of public office or of a merchant family. As we shall see, as a result of social mobility, there could be a considerable movement in and out of such families and so you may find that your own family is at some periods much more easily traceable than at others.

The existence of records is obviously of vital importance in successfully tracing your family history. From time to time records may have been lost, damaged, destroyed or have been kept negligently. Some parish registers begin in the sixteenth century, others not until the eighteenth, which poses considerable problems for the genealogist.

Names, both Christian names and surnames, can range from the very common to the very unusual and an unusual name or combination of names can make a tremendous difference in the ability to identify the individual you are seeking. In city parishes with large numbers of baptisms, marriages and burials, there may be a number of persons of the same name registered at around the same date, given that the name is a fairly common one. On the other hand, if you are searching for an unusual name, there is a much greater chance of a correct identification. Customs for choosing Christian names, particularly in Scotland, can also lend a helping hand to the researcher and are discussed in Chapter 9.

The last of Wagner's factors is that of continuity. A family which has a continuous connection with one place is normally much easier to trace than one which moved about a lot. Movement from place to place often poses problems in family history research. It could take place on a small scale from parish to parish and was often more common than might be imagined. Movement within a ten-mile radius was very common in the past, but a move of a greater distance can be difficult for the family historian to trace. The greatest migration which affected the population as a whole was the movement from the country to the towns during the Industrial Revolution, particularly in the first half of the nineteenth century. Scotland also saw a great influx of Irish immigrants in the nineteenth century, with the largest numbers settling in the Glasgow area but with significant numbers also in Edinburgh and Dundee. There have been other groups of immigrants in the past, but on a very much smaller scale. Continuity can also be evident in a long connection with a particular piece of land, an occupation or an institution. All such connections tend to improve the chance of successful research.

You are unlikely to be blessed with a combination of all these factors and although your family may have been resident in one place for several centuries, you may have the misfortune to discover that the records are poor and only began relatively recently. Perhaps one of the other factors may provide extra assistance.

You may now be asking what are the likely chances of success. Although you may hear of people who claim to be descended from Normans who came over with William the Conqueror, this is extremely unlikely. It seems that no one can prove a continuous descent in the male line from a companion of William at Hastings. There are a handful of very long descents in the male line which have been proved, a good example being the family of Arden, which is descended from Aelfwine, Sheriff of Warwickshire before 1066. In Scotland, the various branches of the family of Dundas can trace their ancestry back to Helias de Dundas, living in the early twelfth century. These descents are exceptional and probably on average you would be fortunate to trace back to the seventeenth century. You should certainly have a good chance of reaching the mid-eighteenth century.

SOCIAL MOBILITY

We have already mentioned in passing the question of noble descents and also social mobility in relation to a family's status. Social mobility in Britain was quite marked in contrast to other parts of Europe. It can involve a decline in status from one extreme to the other or may show movement up and down over the centuries. Some examples can illustrate this point well.

Having researched the late Queen Mother's sixty-four ancestors in the seventh generation back, genealogists discovered that they included two dukes, three earls, a viscount, a baron, a duke's daughter, a marquess's daughter, an earl's daughter, a bishop's daughter, six country gentlemen, a director of the East India Company, a banker, three clergymen, the daughter of a Huguenot refugee, the landlord of the George Inn, Stamford, a London toyman and a London plumber. This research applied to ancestry, but examples can also be found in descents that have been researched. A peerage claim for the barony of Dudley, which was in abeyance from 1757 to 1914, brought to light the fact that the co-heirs in the early nineteenth century, who were all descendants of King Henry VII (d. 1509), consisted of a butcher, a gamekeeper, a toll gate keeper, a baker's wife and a tailor's wife.

One of the authors' ancestry provides an interesting example of social mobility. The author's branch of the Holton family moved to Scotland in the 1880s when his great-grandfather, then working as a commercial traveller, settled in Glasgow. He began his working life as a hosiery warehouseman and came from a family of farmers and butchers in Suffolk. His maternal grandfather, Anthony Hicks, had also been a farmer, but Anthony's mother, Sarah Timperley, although her immediate ancestors were Suffolk farmers, was the third generation in descent from Thomas Timperley, Lord of the Manor of Hintlesham. This family was for several generations closely associated with the Mowbray and Howard Dukes of Norfolk and William Timperley actually married Margaret Howard, an illegitimate daughter of Thomas Howard, 3rd Duke of Norfolk, in the early sixteenth century. The 3rd Duke, who was a major figure in the Court of Henry VIII, was descended, through the Mowbrays, from Thomas of Brotherton, the second son of King Edward I. If you do happen to prove a connection with a royal family, quite amazing ancestors can be traced. For example, Edward I was descended from William the Conqueror, St Margaret of Scotland and the Emperor Charlemagne, while his second wife, Margaret of France, the mother of Thomas of Brotherton, numbered St Louis and Charlemagne amongst her ancestors.

We hope that this chapter has given you some background firstly on the history and uses of genealogy and the importance of family history to other historical studies and secondly on various factors which will affect the course of your own researches.

CHAPTER 1

GATHERING INFORMATION FROM YOUR FAMILY

If you are setting out on the trail of tracing your ancestors and collecting the history of your family, the first step should really be to try to gather as much information as possible that you already know, or that other family members know. You may find that information readily, or you may find that it is tucked away in the recesses of someone's mind, or in the depths of a relative's cupboard or attic.

It would be possible to work back, simply knowing your own name and your date of birth, but this would be a very clinical way of working. You could miss out on the really interesting flesh to be put on the bones of genealogy, the warmth and humour of family life, the anecdotes about the characteristics of members of previous generations.

The first source of information should be yourself and family members. This is an extremely important first step – to try to gather and collate all information from the living relatives to whom you can gain access.

You may be surprised at how much genealogical information is stored in families, once you start to probe a bit further. You may know a surprising amount yourself, when you start to formalise or organise that information. Other family members may have access to invaluable records, certificates, photographs, family recollections, rumours and scandals.

WHEN SHOULD YOU START?

There is really no time like the present. You should be prepared especially to take any suitable opportunity to talk to members of the older generations within your family about their brothers and sisters, parents, aunts, uncles and cousins and take careful note of what they have to tell you. If you postpone the start of this process, then members of the older generation may well have departed, taking all the gems of personal detail about your ancestors with them, never to be recovered.

Of course, you will have to approach the matter with a great deal of tact. If you suddenly ask a relative whom you haven't bothered with for the last twenty years to give you all the most intimate details about the family, to hand over certificates and photographs at the first meeting, you are unlikely to achieve anything apart from instant suspicion of your motives and a permanent refusal to have any further dealings with you! You must try to establish a relationship of mutual trust, genuine interest and concern. This will take time and effort, but can pay huge dividends in the longer run.

WHAT KIND OF MATERIAL ARE YOU LOOKING FOR?

- Names
- Dates
- Places
- Occupations

These may take the more official form of birth certificates, marriage certificates or death certificates. However other less formal or recollected verbal information is worth recording, but should not be accepted as absolutely accurate.

Further information, of a less cold statistical nature, is very useful as you build up a picture of your family history, to find out what made your forebears tick, to trace shared characteristics through the generations, and so on.

Headings (though this is not an exhaustive list) might include:

- Appearance
- Characteristics
- Habits
- Motives
- Odd sayings
- Family legend(s)
- Old photographs
- Memorial cards
- Indentures
- Granny's birthday book
- School reports
- Army rolls of honour
- Family Bible

HOW SHOULD I APPROACH THE GAINING OF INFORMATION FROM RELATIVES?

As stated previously, this has to be done carefully, sympathetically and tactfully. Be careful not to over-tire anyone. Talk about people in the way the relative will know them. Don't press for specific dates, but try to relate to world, national, local or personal events, for example 'The War', or 'when you were at school', or 'before your brother left home'. An unobtrusive voice-recording could be taken, checking first that the interviewee would be comfortable with this, rather than scribbling notes and having to ask for repetition of some detail.

SOME KEYNOTES OF SUCCESS

Don't be in a hurry to go somewhere else, or over-stay your welcome. Try to make them relax; you want them to feel that you are genuinely interested in the other people and themselves. Make a point of recording as much information as possible, including those details that may not seem important at the time, but might turn out to be very helpful later.

A GOOD STRATEGY

Don't visit a relative with a view to gaining all the information you can without offering anything in return. This will immediately arouse suspicion, and you should try to add some information to which you have access, even if that is simply the latest news and pictures of your branch of the current generation.

Some possible items to take with you could be:

- Family photographs
- Mystery pictures
- A small tape-recorder or digital voice-recorder
- An incomplete or **outline family tree** (leaving room for discussion on details)

The big advantage in using a digital voice-recorder compared with a tape-recorder is that many of them now save in MP3 format, which can be saved on a computer, listened to on an MP3 player, stored on a CD or DVD, or included as a 'sound-byte' on a website. The cost of these recorders is becoming very reasonable and, in fact, an increasing number of mobile phones can be used as MP3 players and digital voice-recorders.

A SYSTEM FOR RECORDING THIS INFORMATION

You may or may not decide that taking a small tape-recorder, digital voice-recorder or mobile phone would be suitable for recording information gained during your visit with an elderly relative. No matter what you decide, it is vital that you record in some permanent, readable form all the information that you have already, or have gained during this interview. An example of a family questionnaire form which should cover all the potential areas of interest is given on page 173.

This could be posted to a relative, or could simply be used as a structure to record the results of your meeting. It is important to say at this point that although the bare facts of names, places and dates are very important to build up the structure, or skeleton, of your family history, the anecdotes about relatives are much more enlivening to your new-found interest. It can be quite exciting to hear of the eccentricities, pet likes and dislikes, or sense of humour of someone who previously had just been a name on a yellowing certificate or the subject of a rather staid, sepia photograph.

Information about the existence of other sources of family knowledge, such as a family Bible, or news of a distant cousin also interested in the family, can open up new vistas of possibilities.

At this stage, you shouldn't worry that there are more blanks than completed spaces. It is very likely that the information which you already have, or have been given, isn't completely accurate.

Later on, in Chapter 3, we will show you that there are ways to use your possibly inaccurate information to lead you to reliable sources of accurate dates, and so on.

Another possible means of recording information is an individual record of significant details about one particular relative or ancestor. Depending upon your preference, you may find this easier to handle during an interview. It has the limitation that it does not allow for extra, exciting anecdotes to be added, but caters solely for the bare statistical bones of the individual concerned. Here are some broad headings which could be used:

- First names
- Surname
- When born
- Where born
- When baptised
- Where baptised
- Father's name

- Father's occupation
- Mother's name
- Parents' date of marriage
- Parents' place of marriage
- Date of marriage
- Date of death
- Place of death
- Cause of death

Whatever method you decide to use for keeping your records, it is very important to be methodical and well organised. So many of us involved in family history research have, in our enthusiasm, jotted down notes on different subjects and from different sources all in the same notebook. This soon makes it very much more difficult to locate information than it need be, and it takes a great deal of work to reorganise the data at a later stage. With some careful planning at the outset, this situation can be avoided.

MEANS OF DISPLAYING A FAMILY TREE

THE DROP LINE CHART

You will probably already have seen the most common form of graphically displaying a family tree – in the form of a 'tree' with the twigs and branches decked out with leaves, each leaf representing a family member.

The links back to the common ancestor are shown moving back through the twigs to the larger branches and finally to the trunk. This kind of tree can most commonly be seen in museums representing the genealogy of aristocratic or royal families.

However, a simpler form of this can be seen in the drop line chart.

The oldest generation is shown at the top of the chart, with succeeding generations branching out lower down, with links moving downwards normally through marriage, which is indicated by an 'equals' (=) sign. The same generations can be seen side by side along the same row on the chart. Sometimes if there are many generations and large families, this can demand very wide paper or extremely small, cramped writing. It may be impossible to arrange for all those of the same generation to appear on the same row. The details you include could vary widely from the basic names with dates of birth or baptism, and death or burial, to more elaborate entries with places of birth, marriage and death, date of marriage, occupations, and so on.

Drop line chart

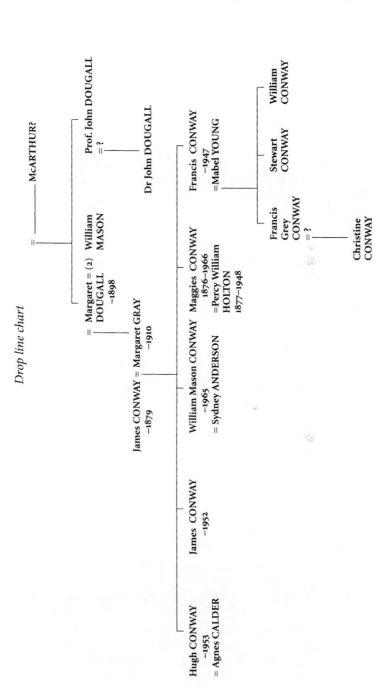

Pedigree or birth brief

1 John Ramsay WINCH
born 1 April 1952
where Johnstone, Renfrewshire
when married 6 July 1979
died

Aileen Anne Elizabeth DUNN

---

2 Henry Thomas WINCH
born 7 February 1910
where Newhaven, Midlothian
when married 26 May 1951
died 16 February 1997

3 Minnie HULSON
born 3 March 1915
where Birmingham
died 6 December 1984

---

4 John Ramsay WINCH
born c. 1883
where Queenborough, Kent
when married 1906
died 1963

5 Euphemia MESSER
born c. 1875
where Edinburgh
died 1965

6 Theophilus HULSON
born
where
when married
died 1923

7 Minnie?
born
where Plymouth?
died

---

8 Henry Thomas WINCH
born
where Queenborough, Kent
when married
died

9 Margaret? Thomson? RAMSAY
born
where Newhaven?
died

10 Robert MESSER
born
where
when married
died

11
born
where
died

12
born
where
when married
died

13
born
where
Died

14
born
where
when married
died

15
born
where
died

PEDIGREE OR BIRTH BRIEF

As you can see in the example given, the pedigree begins on the left-hand side of the page, with one individual.

As you proceed to the right, you move back in time to the parents, grandparents, great-grandparents and so on, with each generation of ancestors arranged in columns. It is possible to have a number of these pedigrees, each beginning with a different individual, to record various lines of ancestors. The limitation is, of course, that it does not accommodate brothers, sisters and their descendants, as the drop line chart does.

THE CIRCULAR TREE

Like the pedigree, this can be a useful starting tool for building up the framework of a family tree. It is limited in that it does not show brothers and sisters, but only parents of one child. You can think of it as a cross-section of a tree-trunk, with succeeding rings radiating outwards.

Normally, you would start out with yourself in the central 'core' of the circle or 'trunk' and move outwards to your mother and father in the next 'shell', then their parents in the succeeding shell, and so on. A number of these charts can be used, with different interesting individuals forming the central core.

This will suffice as a starting place to record your information. As your research starts to build up, we will see that increasingly there are commonly available information technology tools that will help you to keep track of the vast quantities of interesting detail which you will accumulate surprisingly quickly without having to resort to pencil and rubber, screwing up paper and rewriting vast tracts of information.

Circular tree

Family information form

Family Information Form

Please give full names and previous surname(s)

Your Name John Ramsay Winch	**Husband / Wife** Aileen A. E. Dunn
	(& maiden name)
Date & Place of Birth / Baptism	1 April 1952, Johnstone	22 April 1953, Lennoxtown
Date & Place of Marriage	6 July 1979, Lennoxtown	
Date & Place of Death / Burial		
Occupation	University Lecturer	Primary School Teacher

Your Children

	Douglas John	Kirsten Anne	Louise Amy
Date & Place of Birth / Baptism	2 April 1983, Paisley	19 February 1986, Paisley	13 January 1991, Paisley
Date & Place of Marriage			
Name of Husband / Wife			
Date & Place of Death / Burial			
Occupation			

Their Children

1
2
3

Your Father

		Your Mother (& maiden name)
Name	Henry Thomas Winch	Minnie Ethel Theodora Hulson
Date & Place of Birth / Baptism	7 February 1910, Leith	3 March 1915, Birmingham
Date & Place of Marriage	26 May 1951, Birmingham	
Date & Place of Death / Burial	16 February 1997, Renfrew	6 December 1984, Renfrew
Occupation	Draughtsman	Primary School Teacher

Your FATHER's Father

		His Wife (& maiden name)
Name	John Ramsay Winch	Euphemia O? R? Messer
Date & Place of Birth / Baptism	1880s, England?	1875, Edinburgh
Date & Place of Marriage	26 June 1906, where?	
Date & Place of Death / Burial	1963, Paisley	1965, Paisley
Occupation	OSM, Royal Engineers	

Your MOTHER's Father

Name   Theophilus Hulson   **His Wife** (& maiden name)
    Minnie ?

Date & Place of Birth / Baptism   ?

Date & Place of Marriage   ?   ?

Date & Place of Death / Burial   1924, ?   1953, Weston-Super-Mare

Occupation   Admiralty Overseer

Other Family Members

Do you know any other information about other relatives, such as uncles, aunts, great-uncles, great-aunts, cousins, etc.?

1. Full name   Relationship
Details

2. Full name   Relationship
Details

3. Full name   Relationship
Details

Family Traditions

Are there any family traditions / stories that you can recall?
My great-grandfather, called Henry Thomas Winch, lived in Queenborough, Kent and sailed a Thames Barge.

Do you know of the existence of a family Bible? Does it have family details? Where is it?
There is a page torn out of my father's mother's old family Bible with some obscure birth and death dates.

CASE STUDY

The example of a completed family 'questionnaire' or 'information' form given here shows how such a form may look in the early stages of your research. Indeed, this represents the quantity of information which one of the authors had at his disposal at the start of his family history investigations.

You will have taken some time to investigate all of this information by means of family sources and then to document what you have discovered. It would be a pity, therefore, if both old documentary evidence (such as certificates and old photographs) and any new documentation which you have created (such as a draft family tree) were to be at risk of unnecessary deterioration. In Chapter 2 we consider how best to ensure that such materials are preserved.

CHAPTER 2

RECORDING AND STORING INFORMATION

By the time you have carried out some research into your family history at home, with relatives, and at a later stage in the ScotlandsPeople Centre at General Register House in Edinburgh and at local libraries, you will very soon have accumulated quite a considerable quantity of detailed information. Unless you have a systematic way of storing that information, it can very easily become confused and you may misunderstand the links and relationships. Important details can soon be lost or mislaid, especially if you rely on memory alone.

In this chapter we hope to illustrate the pros and cons of methods of storing the harvest of your research, in order that you can keep it secure yet gain ready access to update your family tree in the light of your latest research results.

As a general rule, you should always clearly distinguish between the information you have found in the original sources and the information you have built up based on these sources. The source material should be stored quite separately from your conclusions.

Indeed, you may require to return to your original source material as your own research (or that of future generations) progresses in order to correct or update previous conclusions. Therefore it is most important that this valuable source material is stored in a manner which will help to preserve it.

PAPER RECORDS

You can, of course, simply write the information down on paper. This is, naturally, an improvement on memory, supplemented by notes on scraps of paper. The difficulty which can arise with this is that with further investigation, details can be changed, expanded and deleted. An improvement might be to store information on individuals by means of a sorted card-index system. This would allow for new individuals to be inserted in chronological or alphabetical order, and for additional notes to be added to individual cards.

We have produced some sample forms which could be used as the basis of a paper records system. There are separate sheets for a variety of purposes, and use of these will encourage you to note down the information in a systematic fashion. Examples of these are given in the section 'Sample Forms for Obtaining and recording Information', starting on page 173.

KEEPING TRACK BY COMPUTER

The most significant advantage of using a computer system to assist in the maintenance of your family history research is that many different types of information – narrative, dates, relationships, illustrations, family trees, and so on – can be stored in the one compact space, namely on one computer system supplemented by perhaps a number of CDs or memory sticks.

There are some aspects of your family tree that can never be stored on a computer system. Naturally, original certificates, photographs and papers still need to be stored, preferably in a secure and fireproof cabinet. Though the making of copies can never supplant the thrill of finding and retaining original documents, it is, however, possible to scan copies of the original photographs and documents and store them as graphics files on disk.

In the very gradual process of building up the picture of your family history, the possibility of storing incomplete information which can be added to in a piecemeal fashion, without the need for a complete rewrite of the information, is one of the main strengths of computer use for this purpose. There is the additional benefit that paper copies of the information can be printed out whenever you require, without having to arrange for photocopying or storing large quantities of duplicated paper.

WORD PROCESSING

A word processing system of any variety with which you are familiar is of enormous value to you in the pursuit of building up the narrative of your family history. You can write a partially complete narrative and return to it with amendments and additions at any time as your investigations proceed. In the case of the word processing software produced within the last ten years or so, it is possible to include pictures (or graphics) which can help to enliven your narrative, and to save the illustrated narrative as a word-processed file on disk. If you have old photographs, rather than stick them onto your page, it is possible to use a scanner attached to the computer which will copy them in a suitable form for storage along with your text as part of your word-processed file. It is also possible to enhance the scanned image if the original is somewhat faded. This then allows you to keep the precious original photographs safely filed away for posterity.

USING DATABASES

If, for example, you have lists of census details which may be connected with your family, it will be of value to put them into a database. The fields of the database should follow the different columns in the census enumeration sheet, such as name, relationship to head of household, age, marital status, occupation, and so on. Your collection can then be browsed through, searched, put into different orders and printed out in the order you wish. Another effective use of a database would be to store information which you have gathered from the International Genealogical Index (IGI).

USING SPREADSHEETS

If you simply have a set of information which is best stored in the form of a table, you may find it simpler to use a spreadsheet program such as Microsoft Excel. An example of one use of a spreadsheet can be seen in the case study on page 37.

SPECIALIST GENEALOGICAL SOFTWARE

Some basic requirements for choosing suitable specialist software for storing your family history information are set out below. The program should allow you to record all data that you discover during your research, including conflicting data for the same event, and you should be able to document where each piece of information that you record was obtained.

Some key features to look for in family history software are as follows:

Integrity The program should not create new data by itself. If the program adds data such as a 'married name' the user should have control over the process.

Recording names Adequate space and fields should be available for recording names and there should be a means to record all name variants a person might use in their life.

Recording dates All standard forms of date entries should be accepted and the user should be able to choose the form in which dates are displayed in the program. The program should allow a 'sort date' or other means to control the sorting of data in the program views and reports.

Recording places A facility should be available to record place names.

Recording roles Many events in your database will have more than one participant. Some programs now have tools to link all of those persons to that event and to allow each differing role to be output to narrative reports.

Multiple parents The software should allow linking a child to not only their natural parents but also to adopted parents and handling other non-traditional relationships.

Multiple spouses The software should also allow linking a person to more than one spouse.

Multimedia There should be provisions for linking multimedia objects (photos, sound, video) to individuals and events and to be able to incorporate those images into reports.

Source documentation It will be advantageous to record the source of any information that you enter into your database to provide substantiation for your research and to tell other researchers where they can locate the data that you are reporting. Programs should include the ability to record citation detail which links the event to the source and records the repository where the source was obtained.

Evidence evaluation A provision should exist to enter a 'surety' value so that you can record your judgement about the validity of any data that you enter.

Searching and sorting The software should provide tools to find individuals and to designate subsets of your data for export and for printing.

Research log Your program should give you the ability to record tasks as you discover what needs to be done and to print a useful report to aid your next trip to a repository.

Data import Some programs permit direct import from the databases produced by other software packages and every major genealogy program supports GEDCOM version 5.5 (GEnealogical Data COMmunication), a standard developed to facilitate exchanging computerised genealogical data.

Data export GEDCOM data transfer is limited to only certain data that fits the specification. Since the more sophisticated programs can record data for which no explicit provision is made in the GEDCOM standard, there may be limits to how much of the data recorded in one piece of software can be transferred to another via GEDCOM. At present, there is no alternative to the GEDCOM system for genealogical information exchange.

Report output To aid your research, you may need to be able to produce lists of subsets of people or events as defined by a 'filter'. When you contact a new relative, you may like to be able to provide them with a concise and readable report such as a pedigree or compact descendant chart to show the stage of your research. At the other end of the spectrum, databases can help in the production of reports such as the family history you have been planning to write. You should, for example, be able to create a readable narrative report with a table of contents, footnotes or endnotes to annotate your data, a bibliography, and one or more indexes. Your report should be exported in a format acceptable to the word processor of your choice for final editing. If you include graphical images, the report should include links to the external image files inserted into the proper places in the text.

Web page creation The facility to convert your data to web page (HTML) format and some aids for web page creation are becoming more valuable with the increasing use of the Internet by genealogists.

Backup Your program should have backup capabilities to safeguard your data.

SOFTWARE FOR PC AND WINDOWS

Personal Ancestral File (PAF)

PAF is a 32-bit application that runs under the Windows operating system. A free download is available from http://www.familysearch.org

PAF's Edit Individual screen has sections for Personal (name elements, sex), Events (birth, christening, death, burial), LDS Ordinances (displayed optionally), Other Events (predefined or custom) and Other (name variants, cause of death, physical description and custom ID). A simple marriage record screen records the marriage and has a divorce flag. Other data may go in the individual or marriage note fields. Data in the note fields may be 'regular' (text) or 'tagged' (text denoted by named tags). A leading character may mark notes as printable or confidential.

Name and place fields are limited to 120 characters. The edit individual screen allows for married name, 'also known as' and nickname. Additional names can be entered in the other events section.

Children can be linked to multiple sets of parents and each relationship can be marked as one of five predefined types (biological, adopted, guardian, challenged or disproved). However, you can select only one type of parent link for each set of parents and you can have one type of parent link for any given parent.

Multimedia objects can be added to any individual or source. Default photos optionally display on the Family View screen and can be included on reports and web pages.

One or more sources can be attached to the data and events on the edit individual or marriage screen. Tagged notes can also be entered as events on the edit individual screen with date, place and sources. The source screen allows full source documentation including the repository, citation details, comments, a field for recording full text and an image. A new source or repository needs to be entered only once and existing entries can be selected or edited from master lists. A source with citation details may be 'memorised' and copied to new event entries.

Advanced search tools are available, using wildcards, relationship filters and field filters. Individuals or groups can be selected for reports, GEDCOM export (see 'Data import' on page 25) or editing. For example, a place-spelling error can be easily corrected for all individuals affected. 'Global Search and Replace' is available.

Using 'to do' tags in the note fields allows you to build a collection of research tasks and specific subsets of these tasks may be retrieved with the search tools to generate a report for a repository visit or field trip.

The GEDCOM listing file detailing import errors can be included in the notes of each appropriate individual during the import process. This is a superb feature which greatly simplifies 'clean-up' after import.

A wide variety of reports including pedigree, custom, lists, calendar, family group, ancestry, descendants, book, individual summary and two blank forms (pedigree and family group record) can be generated. Six reports including the two book reports can be saved as Rich Text Format (RTF) files for editing in a word processor. Another Windows program, the PAF Companion, can be used with PAF for printing many of the same reports in differing formats and several additional features such as kinship report, fan chart, charts of ancestors and descendants. PAF includes tools to create web pages. File backup/restore options are available.

Family Tree Maker
Family Tree Maker is a widely used genealogical software package which has been supported by the BBC television series *Who Do You Think You Are?*. It runs on Windows operating systems. Updated versions have so far appeared at regular intervals, with new or amended features.

A person's preferred name, birth, marriage and death facts are entered on the Family Page and are linked to fields on the More About or Facts screen. Unlimited facts for an individual including name variants can be entered on the Facts screen. Each pre-defined or custom fact has fields for fact name, date and a 256-character comment or location detail. Alternative or conflicting facts can be recorded and the preferred alternatives marked. Facts can be sorted alphabetically or chronologically. If a fact text won't fit into the comments/location field, the text is added to the person's notes field. Some information is recorded on other screens (title, alias, address, medical information, and so on). Each marriage has a Facts screen where marriage (or other facts linked to both spouses) and marriage status are recorded, and a Notes screen. Other parents for a child can be added with the Other Parents option and the nature of the relationships is shown on the Lineage screen. Unlimited multimedia objects can be linked to an individual with the 'scrapbook'.

One or more sources can be linked to each fact, but there is no way to link sources to text in the notes fields or to fields on the other screens. Source citation screens for each fact include citation details and the footnote used in narrative reports. Source screens include source details and fields for source location and quality.

Research progress and tasks are recorded in the Research Journal, which can be sorted in one or two columns and printed. Family Tree Maker can import GEDCOM files, older Family Tree Maker files and PAF 2.x/3.0 files. It can export several versions of Family Tree Maker and GEDCOM files.

Only basic search and selection tools are included but a variety of list reports using subsets of the complete file and custom reports can be generated. As would be expected, a variety of narrative reports and charts can be printed. The 'trees' include a unique hourglass tree showing both an individual's ancestors and descendants and an all-in-one tree. Publication tools include three styles of genealogy report and a 'family book'. Several narrative reports can be exported to text or RTF files for editing. Family Tree Maker includes tools for publishing to the Internet and space is available for users on the Family Tree Maker website.

Family Tree Maker creates backup files in the locations of your choice, on your hard disk, on CD or on memory stick.

SOFTWARE FOR MACINTOSH

Reunion
Reunion is a complete, elegant, robust and flexible genealogy software program for the Macintosh and is the only one commercially available for use on Macintosh systems. At the time of writing, the latest version is Reunion 9. It helps you to document, store and display information about your family history. It can record names, dates, places, facts, plenty of notes, sources of information, pictures, sound and video. It produces high-quality charts and other types of document. Some of its main features include the creation of large graphic tree charts including descendant charts up to 99 generations and pedigree charts up to 35 generations. It also permits GEDCOM import/export. Other facilities include the production of comprehensive listings, which could support the writing of family histories. Full on-screen editing of box colour, font, font size, shadow, border, connecting lines and captions is permitted. A large variety of reports and forms is offered. Reunion provides indexes, event calendars, family group sheets, family histories, register reports, Ahnentafel reports, person sheets, questionnaires,

mailing lists, birthday lists, and can calculate relationships, ages, life expectancies and other statistics. It permits storage of up to 30,000 characters of text per person, in note format. The Ahnentafel system allows for the numbering of ancestors beginning with a descendant. This system allows one to derive an ancestor's number without compiling the list and allows one to derive an ancestor's relationship based on their number.

The number of a person's father is the double of their own number, and the number of a person's mother is the double of their own, plus one. For instance, if the number of John Smith is 10, his father is 20, and his mother is 21.

The first fifteen numbers, identifying individuals in four generations, are as follows:

1   Subject
2   Father
3   Mother
4   Father's father
5   Father's mother
6   Mother's father
7   Mother's mother
8   Father's father's father
9   Father's father's mother
10   Father's mother's father
11   Father's mother's mother
12   Mother's father's father
13   Mother's father's mother
14   Mother's mother's father
15   Mother's mother's mother

Some of the pieces of software described above have a variety of versions, perhaps described as 'Deluxe' or 'Grande Suite'. Be wary of some of these more expensive versions – at extra expense to you they may contain a large number of CDs of additional census information and other records which may be of very little value to you, especially if the CDs contain information pertaining only to the United States or Canada. More helpfully, you may see some offered for sale specifically marked as 'UK version' or 'European edition'.

With any one of these PC or Macintosh family history software programs and properly disciplined work habits, a person could do a reasonable job of recording and documenting their family history.

The more sophisticated programs give a researcher more choice over their data recording and more control over report output, at the expense of an accompanying increase in program complexity and a steeper learning curve.

For a more comprehensive list of commercially available and 'shareware' genealogical software and also for up-to-date reviews, you could refer to Cyndi's List on the Internet.

VOICE RECORDING (DIGITAL OR AUDIO CASSETTE)

Recollections of an elderly relative can be a rich source of family history, forming a living link with past generations. It is just possible that you may be in touch with a personal recollection of an ancestor who was born 150 years ago. Recollections may be more colourful when recorded: they may be in a dialect which is fast disappearing; the narrator may mimic the way in which the story was originally told; and a whole lot of narrative colour can be added to an otherwise fairly sterile piece of family history. As mentioned in Chapter 1, you may find it more valuable to use a digital voice-recorder or the digital voice-recording facility of a mobile phone in order that the recording can be stored on computer and played either via the computer or an MP3 player.

VIDEO RECORDING

Local history
If you are able to visit the area from which your ancestors came, then the use of a camera, or better still a digital video recorder, can capture the feeling of those surroundings. An illustration of a house where someone lived, the village, the local church, prominent buildings, local occupations and, for the more morbid amongst us, gravestones, can enliven your family history when you prepare it for consumption by other interested parties.

Family gatherings
If a family gathering is held, it can be quite enlightening to record members attending, especially if it is a large gathering covering a number of generations and involving quite distant cousins. Family characteristics can be noted in reviewing the video recording, and shared characteristics between groups of family members can be linked with photographs and recollections of particular significant ancestors.

PRESERVATION OF MATERIALS

The original materials which you have assembled, your source materials, are the most valuable assets in your collection – upon these the construction of your family tree and history will depend; in the light of new source material an expanded or amended history will be developed. As computers develop very rapidly and as software changes, in the longer term information and images stored on computer can become obsolete if left unattended for a number of years. Therefore it is most important that you do everything possible to ensure that such original materials are conserved in the best condition possible – both for your own future use and that of future generations.

Such materials can be considered as archives and can include papers, plans, photographs and other media. There are specific standards for the preservation of archives, such as British Standard 5454: Storage and exhibition of archival documents, and A Standard for Record Repositories (Royal Commission on Historical Manuscripts, second edition, 1997). For practical reasons very few private individuals will be able to meet all of these professional recommendations, but attention to some guidelines will help you to minimise the risks of deterioration or destruction posed to your source materials or archives. Prevention is usually better than having to try to effect a cure, and by following basic preservation measures you can help to protect your materials for future generations. Conservation treatments can be expensive, and not all damage is reversible. Features of good archive preservation are addressed below under the following headings: Accommodation, Security, Environment and storage, Reprography and Disasters.

Accommodation

- Should be soundly constructed of brick, stone or concrete, with adequate protection against damp or unauthorised entry.
- Should be dedicated to that purpose, as far as possible – for example, not part of a children's play area.
- Should be supplied with a carbon dioxide fire extinguisher, in accordance with the advice of the local fire service.

Where possible, the following locations should be avoided:

- Garages and garden huts.
- Attics and basements, owing to the risks of water ingress and the difficulty of evacuating them in the case of an emergency.

- Flat roofs, which are liable to leak.
- Ground-floor rooms, which are more vulnerable to intruders.
- Where there is plumbing, drainage or guttering nearby.
- Where there is excessive light, in the proximity of windows or skylights.
- Near to gas and electrical appliances, which are potential fire hazards.
- Near to chimneys, as they may provide a route for damp.

Security

- If papers are stored in accommodation which is also used for other purposes, the cupboard in which they are stored should be locked.
- When tradespeople are working around the area, the archives should be removed or the working practices adapted, ideally under supervision.
- You should control access to your materials, and keep a notebook in which access by others to your materials is recorded. Materials given out should be carefully checked beforehand and on their return.
- You should try to ensure that the materials are fully covered by any domestic intruder alarm system.

Environment and storage

In addition to providing sound and secure accommodation, archive materials also require a stable environment and suitable storage conditions if their safety is to be assured. Over a period of years, unsuitable environments have proved to be a main cause of damage to archives. If the environment is too dry, the documents may become brittle; dampness and poor ventilation may encourage the growth of mould; high temperatures may speed up the deterioration process. In general, a consistent cool atmosphere with adequate ventilation is desirable.

- It is likely that your collection of materials will include paper, photographs and other media and should be stored between 13 and 18°C and 55 to 65 per cent relative humidity. Temperature and humidity swings are potentially damaging.
- Where there are windows or skylights, the damaging effects of light can be reduced by the use of blinds or shutters.
- Shelving should be adjustable and at least 15cm above the ground,

and away from windows and external walls owing to the risk of water penetration.

- Papers should be stored in suitable archive boxes. Metal deed boxes are not recommended as they are heavy, liable to rust and will retain water in the event of flooding.
- Volumes should be put on the shelves either upright or flat, never on their fore-edges.
- Separate protection (such as wrapping in acid-free paper) should be given to outsize volumes, documents and maps.
- Loose photographs should be boxed and, where possible, put in polyester sleeves.
- Inspect the store regularly for signs of water penetration, mould growth, insect infestation, and so on.
- Keep the storage area clean and free of waste and rubbish, as dust and organic materials provide an ideal environment for vermin, insects and mould.
- Don't put original documents on permanent display, either in frames or cases, as this can lead to irreversible brittleness and fading.

Reprography

It is essential to maintain a copy of your most important documents and materials. Despite the most careful precautions, damage can occur.

However, **Photocopying** may physically damage or fade archives. The following types of material should never be photocopied:

- fragile or damaged documents
- parchment
- outsize documents and volumes
- original photographs
- documents with seals attached
- tightly bound volumes
- volumes with decorative or historical bindings

Photography on your own premises is usually a suitable alternative to photocopying, and will provide a negative for future use. The details are a bit technical for the amateur photographer, but nevertheless lighting guidance is crucial, as follows:

- Lighting should not exceed 1,000 lux, under tungsten lighting.
- If metallic halide lamps are used, this may be increased to 2,500 lux.

- Flash photography is acceptable under certain circumstances: the upper limit for flash photography is 20 lux-minutes or f22 on 100ASA film or equivalent.
- A UV filter over each flash is desirable.

It is important to remember that copyright issues must be respected.

Disasters

- Take increased precautions during periods of increased risk, such as building renovation and bad weather.
- Turn off and/or disconnect all inessential utilities when the premises are unoccupied.
- Arrange comprehensive insurance for the costs of salvage and conservation for your archives.

In the unfortunate event of a disaster you should remain calm and take no risks. Some pointers, while still prioritising your personal safety, are as follows:

- Protect all papers at risk but as yet undamaged with polythene sheeting or move them to another secure location.
- Establish a sorting area for your salvaged material.
- Clear first papers that have fallen on the floor.
- When clearing shelves, start at the top and work down for safety reasons.
- Where possible, remove materials from the storage area in order; if reference numbers are used, evacuated archive material should be labelled with such. If you must write on an original document, use a soft (2B) pencil, not ink.
- Do not attempt to stack boxes if they are wet, as they may disintegrate, causing damage to the contents.
- Remove and replace all damaged boxing. Check first to find out if the contents need drying, as re-boxing damp material will cause serious mould problems in a short period of time, leading to the loss of papers.
- Affected material should be laid out to dry on absorbent paper. Where necessary, clean blotting paper should be used to dry individual documents or placed between the leaves of damp volumes.
- Wet items should be treated within forty-eight hours to avoid mould growth.

- In the event of extensive water damage, wet items (excluding photographic material) may be frozen in a domestic freezer. This action should prevent further deterioration in the documents before they can be assessed by a professional conservationist.

Books

- Do not attempt to open or close wet books.
- Damp books can be dried by cold air from fans after being opened and stood on end. Check periodically, and turn them head to tail to prevent sagging and damage to bindings.

Bundles, loose papers and files

- Where masses of papers are found stuck together, there should be no attempt to separate them, as this will lead to removal of print.
- Do not attempt to flatten folded items, as this will lead to tearing.
- Some single-leaf items may be suitable for air-drying.

Photographic material

- Wet photographs will begin to disintegrate and develop mould if left in piles. Wherever possible, air-dry them. Lay out photographs (including glass plates) on absorbent paper, emulsion side up for air-drying. Seek expert advice as soon as possible.
- Water-damaged microforms should be immersed in buckets of clean cold water until they can be reprocessed.

A photographic record of your affected archive material can assist when negotiating claims with your insurers.

If all such measures have failed or you receive material in a damaged condition, the National Archives of Scotland's Conservation Unit can be contacted to advise on commercially available conservation services.

CASE STUDY

The service record of John Ramsay Winch illustrated here may give you an idea of the kind of information you may wish to collate, by means of a word processor. It shows information about an ancestor's military record collected from a variety of family recollections, sources and documents.

Service record as recorded on a word processor

The Service Record of John Ramsay Winch:

No. 2204213

From	To	Rank	Details
7 February 1903	3 April 1908		Imperial Yeomanry or Voluntary Force: Forth Division Sub-Marine Miners RE
1 August 1904	28 Feb 1909	2nd Crpl	Forth Division RE (Vol.) Electrical Engineers
1 March 1909	16 August 1909	Corpl	
17 August 1909	16 May 1911	Sergeant	
17 May 1911	31 Dec 1913		Renfrewshire (F) RE
1 January 1914		CSM	

Embodied Service

5 August 1914			406th Field Company RE
4? August 1914	17 Dec 1915		Home Forces
18 Dec 1915	25 April 1916		British Expeditionary Force – Egypt
26 April 1916			British Expeditionary Force – France
7 November 1917			'Specially mentioned' in Sir Douglas Haig's Despatch, *London Gazette*
2 December 1917			Ph II Order No. 2, gassed
17 June 1918			Meritorious Service Medal, *vide London Gazette* d. 17/6/18
21 June 1919	25 June 1919		5th Prov. Company No. 27
26 June 1919	12 August 1919		Home Forces
9 September 1919			Disembodied on demobilisation at Chatham
31 March 1920			Discharged on demobilisation, para 392 (XXVIII) KR

Re-enlisted Service

13 April 1921			'F' (Hld) Renfrew Field Company RE
31 May 1921		Instr'r	Discharged on enlistment in the Regular Army on appointment as Instructor
1 June 1921		Sapper	51st The Highland Division (T) RE
2 June 1921		Sergeant	Promoted authy ACS 337/21 to GOC 51st (Hld) Division A1/835 on 23/4/21
28 August 1922		A/CSM	Warrant Officer Class II
30 March 1923			Service for one year approved
8 May 1924			Service for a further period of one year approved
8 May 1925			Service for a further period of one year approved
11 February 1926			Service for a further period of one year approved
....			Left Drill Hall, joined RE 'Old Comrades'
1929			Clasp to Territorial Efficiency Medal
1939	1945		Home Guard, Bomb Disposal Squad, on disbandment made up to Lieutenant

Alternatively, you may find it easier to use a spreadsheet (such as Microsoft Excel) if your information more readily falls into categories which have fairly brief descriptions, such as in the example given of Newhaven fishing vessels:

Information recorded in a spreadsheet

Reg. #		Name	Date	Description	Other Details
LH	82	May Queen	1887	Steam Screw Schooner	
LH	190	Perseverance	1900	Decked Mainsail, Jib & Foresail	Nets, N/L dredge
LH	749	Joan	1886	O/B Lug Sail	
LH	781	Three Sisters	1886	O/B Lug Sail, 25ft, 5 tons, 5 crew	reg 1875
LH	874	Two Sisters	1886	O/B Lug N/L, 5 tons, 3 crew	reg 1877
LH	909	Hope			
LH	978	Reaper		Clinker 2/Lug, 47ft, 6 tons, 4 crew	motorised 1921
LH	985	William & Margaret		27ft, 5 tons, 4 crew	reg. after engine 1920/23
LH	210	The Reliance	1928	Last boat built in the Fisherman's Park, Newhaven	

To keep your family tree in some organised form, you may wish to use a piece of software specifically designed to keep track of the relationships and links between generations of your family tree, together with some details of dates and other 'structural' information. The 'information card' example given here shows a screen of information from a specific piece of family history software (or genealogical database in this case Reunion for Macintosh), showing some more structural information from the family in the preceding examples. You will notice that the information on this 'card' is in a structured and summary form related primarily to births, marriages, deaths and occupations, and so on.

On the other hand, more detail of different types of information (such as an army record or medals) can be included in the word-processed or spreadsheet document. The purposes of both are complementary to each other, the family history software providing a means of maintaining and updating the correct links and order across the generations as research progresses.

Information card from a family history software program

Henry Thomas WINCH	Robert MESSER	
1849 - 1899	1852 - 1931	
Margaret Thomson RAMSAY	Jane ROBERTSON	
1859 - 1923	1851 - 1930	

Grandfather 26 Jun 1906, St Cuthbert's Parish Church, Edinburgh Grandmother

John Ramsay WINCH	**Euphemia Galloway Robertson MESSER**
Birth	8 Nov 1883	Birth	21 Oct 1875
	Queenborough, Kent, England		13 Ponton Street, Edinburgh, Scotland
Death	6 Jan 1963 Age: 79	Death	3 Mar 1965 Age: 89
	36 Windsor Crescent, Paisley, Scotland		36 Windsor Crescent, Paisley, Scotland
Occ	Company Sergeant Major, Royal Engineers - 406 Fi	Occ	Housewife
Educ		Educ	
Reli	Episcopal Church	Reli	Episcopal Church
Note	He received 5 or 6 medals in World War 1,	Note	
	namely:		
	Meritorious Service Medal		
	Territorial Force Efficiency Medal (clasp in 1929)		
	British War Medal, 1914-20		
ID: 13	Changed: 28 Nov 2000	ID: 14	Changed: 15 Jan 2000

Jean Ramsay	Marguerite Thomson

Henry Thomas	Robert Messer

10

CHAPTER 3

BASIC SOURCES FOR FAMILY HISTORY

In this chapter we seek to help you to find more information about your family history, once you have exhausted all the sources you have available in your family. At this stage the next step is to look into the documentary evidence available in official documents. The most important store of information for the new family history researcher is the ScotlandsPeople Centre. Based at the east end of Princes Street, Edinburgh, it gives access via computer to the official Scottish Civil Registers, the census returns for 1841 to 1901, the 'Old' Parish Registers, wills and testaments from 1513 to 1901, coats of arms from 1672 to 1908, and some minor records detailing the register of births, deaths and marriages where it appears that one of the child's parents or the deceased was usually resident in Scotland. At the time of writing, free introductory two-hour taster sessions are available for up to 36 people from 10:00 to 12:00 and from 14:00 to 16:00 on weekdays. The centre opened fully in January 2009; the search fee for the centre is £10 (VAT exempt) for a full or part day, on any weekday between 09:00 and 16:30. It is possible to print off historical records for a small charge per page, save to a memory stick for a charge per image or order entries from the Register of coats of arms for a fixed charge. Should you be unable to travel to Edinburgh, it is also possible to access some of this information via the ScotlandsPeople website (http://www.scotlandspeople.gov.uk) or by means of a CD-ROM – and the Ancestry website also provides access to census returns.

BIRTHS, MARRIAGES AND DEATHS SINCE 1855

If you were born in Scotland, one of your parents probably registered your details with the local registrar, registering the birth. A similar system applies to marriages, whether the ceremony is carried out in a church or in a registry office, and also to deaths.

Since 1 January 1855 in Scotland, the state has assumed responsibility for the logging of the births, marriages and deaths of its citizens. The outcome of all this bureaucracy has been that a vast store of all the original entries since then has been indexed, maintained and made relatively accessible to you, as a member of the general public, for a reasonable fee.

Before we proceed to tell you of the procedure for gaining access to this treasure trove of information, we will give you a few notes on what each type of certificate contains, and what to look out for when you get to look at the actual entries.

The **birth certificate** will give you, in addition to the details you already know about the person's name and sex:

- The date and place of birth even down to the time of the baby's delivery. You should make special note of the address as later on when we look at census returns, you will see that it can be a link to other interesting information.
- The parents' details – names, occupations, the mother's maiden name, and the really valuable information about the date and place of the parents' marriage.
- The name of the informant. This is not normally of importance as it is usually the father or mother. However, if it is not, take a note of it as it may point to a relative which can come in useful in later research.

If you happen to have a birth in 1855, you have struck lucky as it will provide you with information about the number of other children of the marriage at the time of the birth, together with the age and birthplace of the father and mother. Because of the burden of collecting this extra information, this practice was, unfortunately for the family historian, dropped after one year. The reaction against this was particularly sharp between 1856 and 1860, as birth certificates did not include details of the parents' marriage. However, this valuable information was reintroduced in 1861.

The **marriage certificate** will be even more fruitful as it contains information about two people, as follows:

- Where and when the marriage took place. If the ceremony was a religious one, it will tell you by which rites it was performed. This is not something to gloss over as it may point to a family tradition of church-going which could open up other sources of information later on.

- The name, occupation, condition (bachelor or widower), age and address of the bridegroom. Additionally it provides the name and occupation of the father, and the name and maiden name of the mother. This information is vital to taking a step back to the previous generation in your family tree.
- The equivalent details for the bride.
- The names of the witnesses to the signing of the marriage register. Most of the time this will be of little practical use, but take a note of them as it could be a clergyman, a friend or relative of the bride or groom – you never know when this will provide a key to your later researches.

The Scottish **death certificate** is a very valuable document in building up a family tree, unlike its English counterpart. It will tell you:

- The name and occupation of the person whose death has been registered. Sometimes this occupational information is important as it may have changed from the earlier entries in the children's birth certificates, marriage certificate, and so on. Of course, if the deceased was well on in years, the informant may well not be too clear about the actual occupation.
- Marriage details. Again this is valuable information, especially where it refers to a marriage other than the one you had known about previously.
- Where the death occurred. When this happens away from home, the regular address is provided, except for the period between 1856 and 1860. Such addresses should be noted, both from the point of view of simply knowing where the people lived, and to allow you to access census information at a later stage in your research.
- The person's age. This is not always accurate, but can be a reasonable guide to enable you to trace a birth entry in the registers.
- The names of both parents, and also the occupation of the father and maiden name of the mother. This information is the vital link which is missing from the English death certificate, and can enable you to take the all-important step backwards in your family tree. However, again dependent upon the age of the deceased, such names and occupations can sometimes be less than accurate.
- The cause of death, which can be a bit technical but worth recording. Sometimes the duration of the illness is also mentioned.
- The signature of the informant. The name of the person notifying

the death can be more valuable for the family history researcher than the names of the informant on other certificates. It can help you to assess the reliability of the information, as referred to earlier. Further, it can provide useful genealogical information. For instance, if a Janet Messer (maiden name Robertson) has a death certificate signed by Thomas Meikle, brother-in-law, you can deduce that she has at least one sister, who had married a man called Thomas Meikle – not too bad for a small column at the end of a death certificate.

THE CENSUS RECORDS, 1841 TO 1901

Just as the state had taken over responsibility for keeping track of births, marriages and deaths since 1855, it also became concerned with keeping details of the entire population and keeping track of its whereabouts. Since 1801 in Scotland, every ten years a census of the population has been taken, with the exception of 1941. However, only the statistical details have generally been retained for the censuses from 1801 to 1831, and therefore they are not of much use to the family historian.

The full returns for every household for the seven censuses from 1841 to 1901 are available for inspection at the ScotlandsPeople Centre in Edinburgh. Images of the returns can be viewed on computer screen. Later census returns will not be made available to the general public until they are 100 years old, as they may contain some information about a living person which they would not wish to be released publicly. Increasingly, in order to make access easier, local libraries are obtaining copies related to their own parts of the country.

Census returns perhaps hold the greatest amount of information for the ancestor hunter and all the publicly available censuses can be searched on computer by the name of the person you are seeking.

WHAT CAN YOU GLEAN FROM CENSUS RETURNS?

In **1841**, the census asked for a limited amount of information – names, approximate ages rounded down to the nearest five years, occupations, and whether the person was born in the county or not. For those under the age of 15, allegedly exact ages are given.

In **1851**, questions being asked were names, relationships to the person designated as head of the household, precise ages and the actual parish of birth, if in Scotland.

By the time we reach **1891**, a number of extra and quite revealing questions were being asked, such as the ability to speak Gaelic,
the number of rooms being shared by families, and evidence of
disabilities.

The big benefit which the census returns bring to the family
history researcher is to provide complete or partially complete family
groupings in the one place. This could enable you to find brothers
and sisters and perhaps other relatives. However, the absence of one
expected person is no guarantee that they are deceased – they could
have been away from home on business or staying with a friend on
that particular census night! The census return will also provide you
with information on the social circumstances of your ancestors.
Don't neglect to take a look at the details of the neighbours. It may
be useful to note down who is sharing a front door, or a close, with
your ancestors, or living in the neighbouring farm. Census returns
can tell you a lot about the activities of a locality.

SOME PITFALLS

One drawback of census returns is that if you do not know where
your family was living on the night of the census, it may be difficult
to identify the correct entry, particularly if the name is a common
one.

1881 census return for North Leith

(Census for North Leith, 1881 – CEN 1881, 692(1))
26 James Place, Newhaven

Name	Position	Status	Age	Occupation	Birthplace
John Ramsay	Head	Married	48	Fisherman	Born Newhaven
Maryann Ramsay	Wife		40		Born Newhaven
John Ramsay	Son		22	Fisherman	Born Newhaven
William Ramsay	Son		4	Scholar	Born Newhaven

The example of a census entry from our own research revealed
a hitherto unknown much younger son, of age 4. There is also the
possibility that this was an illegitimate son of one of the daughters of
the family, as such arrangements to cover up a family disgrace were
not unknown at the time.

The interesting social background provided by the detail contained in the 1891 census can be seen from the extract from one
address. Amongst other things, the living conditions, particularly of

Details for one address from the 1891 census

Street	Name	Relation	Status	Age	Occupation	Birthplace	Rooms
Williamsburgh 1	HEANEY, Rosean	Head	Widow	50		Ireland	2
Williamsburgh 1	HEANEY, Peter	Son	Unmarried	26	Gardener	Renfrew-shire Houston	
Williamsburgh 1	HEANEY, James	Son	Unmarried	24	Engineer Patternmaker	Renfrew-shire Houston	
Williamsburgh 1	HEANEY, Sarah	Daughter	Unmarried	19	Miliners Shopwoman	Renfrew-shire Houston	
Williamsburgh 1	HEANEY, Alexander	Son	Unmarried	15	Apprentice Mill Mechanic	Stirling-shire Baldernock	
Williamsburgh 1	CHALMERS, Alexander	Head	Married	34	Wood Sawyer	Fife-shire Markinch	2
Williamsburgh 1	HARKNESS, Isabella	Wife	Married	34		Ayr-shire Kirkoswald	
Williamsburgh 1	CHALMERS, William	Son		8	Scholar	Renfrew-shire Paisley	
Williamsburgh 1	CHALMERS, Jessie M K	Daughter		7	Scholar	Renfrew-shire Paisley	
Williamsburgh 1	CHALMERS, James	Son		5	Scholar	Renfrew-shire Paisley	
Williamsburgh 1	CHALMERS, Catherine Herd	Daughter		2		Renfrew-shire Paisley	
Williamsburgh 1	CHALMERS, Isabella Harkness	Daughter		1m		Renfrew-shire Paisley	
Williamsburgh 1	GANSON, Elizabeth	Head	Widow	54	Housekeeper	Ireland	3
Williamsburgh 1	GANSON, William	Son	Unmarried	19	Army Militia Staff	Renfrew-shire Paisley	
Williamsburgh 1	GANSON, George	Son	Unmarried	17	Tailor's Apprentice	Renfrew-shire Paisley	
Williamsburgh 1	JACK, Kate	Daughter	Married	20	Warehouse Worker	East India British Subject	3
Williamsburgh 1	JACK, James	Son in Law	Married	24	Tailor	Renfrew-shire Paisley	
Williamsburgh 1	JACK, Maggie	Grand Daughter		3		Renfrew-shire Paisley	
Williamsburgh 1	JACK, George	Grand Son		1		Renfrew-shire Paisley	
Williamsburgh 1	SHAW, David	Head	Married	53	Power Loom Tenter	Renfrew-shire Neilston	3
Williamsburgh 1	SHAW, Mattie	Wife	Married	52	Power Loom Tenter's Wife	Renfrew-shire Paisley	
Williamsburgh 1	SHAW, David	Son	Unmarried	28	Wool Cloth Miller	Renfrew-shire Paisley	
Williamsburgh v	SHAW, Robert	Son	Unmarried	24	Packing Box Maker	Renfrew-shire Paisley	
Williamsburgh 1	SHAW, Margaret	Daughter	Unmarried	21	Housekeeper	Renfrew-shire Paisley	
Williamsburgh 1	SHAW, William	Son	Unmarried	19	Flesher	Renfrew-shire Paisley	
Williamsburgh 1	SHAW, Mary	Daughter	Unmarried	17	Thread Mill Worker	Renfrew-shire Paisley	
Williamsburgh 1	SHAW, Jessie	Daughter	Unmarried	15	Thread Mill Worker	Renfrew-shire Paisley	
Williamsburgh 1	SHAW, Hepsey	Daughter		12	Scholar	Renfrew-shire Paisley	
Williamsburgh 1	SHAW, John	Son		10	Scholar	Renfrew-shire Paisley	

the Shaw family – ten people living in a three-roomed house – are worthy of note, as an interesting insight into the social history of the area.

OLD PARISH REGISTERS

As you move back in time in the search for your family roots, you will reach the period before Civil Registration (1855) and the earliest useful census (1841). The most important source for you now will be the Old Parish Registers (OPRs). These are the registers of baptisms or births, marriages or the proclamations of banns and burials or deaths, kept in each Church of Scotland parish, of which there are about 900. There is no standard date at which these began and their starting date as well as the way in which they were kept was very much dependent on each individual parish minister. The earliest Parish Registers in Scotland begin in 1553, but only a few date back to the sixteenth century and many began in the eighteenth century. There are some which commenced only in the early nineteenth century and there are even a few places without Parish Registers. Many lack burial or death registers. In theory, all the registrations should have been made in the Parish Registers, but in practice, they are far from complete. Those who were members of other churches, such as the Catholic Church, may not have registered these events in the Church of Scotland registers. Perhaps they will be recorded in registers kept by their own church (see Nonconformist Records in Chapter 7), or not recorded at all. It is always best to consult the OPRs first, however, since many nonconformists will be registered there, plus they are much more easily accessible and searchable.

Another factor affecting the completeness of these registers was the huge growth of the population in the towns from the end of the eighteenth century. With the movement of population, people's ties with the Church could become tenuous and it was not so likely that registrations would be made. In addition, from 1783 to 1794 a stamp duty of threepence was payable by anyone registering an event in the Parish Registers. This seriously affected the number of registrations made.

For example, John McPhail and Florence McArthur were married in 1787 at Glasgow High Church, but Florence's baptism does not seem to have been recorded, although her brother Duncan's baptism appears in 1773. We know from his Will that he had several other brothers and sisters, but only some have been traced in the OPRs.

When considering the amount of information found in the Parish Registers, the first thing to say is that there is normally a good deal less than you would have found in the Civil Registers. Baptisms are likely to give the name and date of baptism of the child, his parents' names, their residence and possibly the father's occupation. Marriage entries usually refer to the proclamation of marriage which was made in the parishes of both the bride and groom. It is possible that more information may be given in one Parish Register than the other and sometimes there is a statement that the marriage did actually take place, with the date. In most cases, the names of the bride and groom, their residences and the date of proclamation are given. Burials will often mention little more than the name of the deceased and the date of burial.

Although this is the information which you might expect to find, it is possible that, in a parish with an interested and conscientious minister, various other details may be included. Quite often the mother's maiden name is given in baptismal entries and godparents' names may also be mentioned. Since these were very often relatives, this could be useful. The actual date of birth might also be given. Additional information found in marriage registers could be parents' names and the occupation of the groom, but almost certainly not ages, which is a great pity from the genealogist's point of view. Burials might give the age of the individual, the cause and date of death and parents' names in the case of a young child. If the deceased's spouse was still alive, his or her name could be included, and if the deceased was a widow or widower, again this might be specified.

Given the comparative lack of information included in the OPRs, one of the major difficulties encountered is the problem of identifying the person you are looking for. Common names, particularly in the towns and Highland parishes, and the frequent use of the same few Christian names in the same family, can make it very difficult to decide who is who, if there is no additional evidence, such as ages or occupations. All you can do in such cases is gather all the information available from every possible source to assist you in making a positive identification.

The searching of the OPRs has been made much easier by the provision of various indexes, including the IGI (International Genealogical Index), described in Chapter 4, although the IGI does not generally include burials and deaths. There are computerised indexes to the baptisms, marriages and burials available on the ScotlandsPeople website and in the ScotlandsPeople Centre. The computer index can be searched for the whole of Scotland or by a particular county and there is also a microfiche version available in family history centres of the Mormon Church and in some libraries.

Having found a reference in the indexes which seems relevant, you can then look at the full entry on a computer screen. It is disappointing not to be able to consult these documents from the time of your ancestors, but as genealogy is so popular now, the necessity of preservation has to come first.

MAKING USE OF THE SCOTLANDSPEOPLE CENTRE

The Centre, located within General Register House at the east end of Princes Street, Edinburgh, is normally open between 09:00 and 16:30, from Monday to Friday, apart from public holidays. The ScotlandsPeople Centre website (http://www.scotlandspeoplehub. gov.uk) gives up-to-date details of charges and procedures for searching amongst the records which they make available to the general public. Having paid your fee, you will be allocated a desk, complete with computer terminal and instructions. It is normally advisable to write in pencil as opposed to pen and no smoking or drinking is allowed, but there is a café within the building and there are plenty of refreshment places of all descriptions within a very short walk. The public search room is located under the dome of the building, designed by the famous Scots architect Robert Adam, and it is a bright, airy place to spend a day searching the records.

Preparation before you go is essential. You should try to establish a number of lines of enquiry before you go, in order to make the fullest use of your valuable day beside the records. We would recommend taking a notebook, or loose-leaf binder, filled with some of the skeletal forms we suggest using, examples of which start on page 177.

The indexes of births, marriages and deaths are now all on computer, as are the indexes for the 1841 to 1901 censuses, the OPRs and the Catholic Church records, all linked to images of the full entries. The instructions for using these systems are fairly simple, and shouldn't prove too daunting. You can carry out a search for a particular name over all of Scotland or restricted to certain areas. An advantage of the Centre is the access it gives to all registered births, marriages and deaths up to the present day.

It is worth noting that there is a Registrar's Office in Park Circus, Glasgow, which gives public access to the computer index of the Civil Registers. However, the digitised entries on computer accessed there only cover the area centred around Glasgow which used to be called Strathclyde Region. Nevertheless, this is a useful addition to the service provided by the ScotlandsPeople Centre in Edinburgh.

This office also provides access to the 1871 to 1901 census returns. There is also a similar facility at the Registrar's Office in Dundee, which covers a variety of statutory records for Dundee, Angus and Tayside, and Old Parish Registers for Tayside.

SCOTLANDSPEOPLE WEBSITE

Access to many of the indexes of the General Register Office for Scotland is available online via the ScotlandsPeople website, with payment being made by credit or debit card. One payment for credits will allow you to search the indexes within a period of 90 consecutive days and to view up to 30 pages, each of which contains a maximum of 15 records. Additional credits are used for viewing images.

At present the database includes the following indexes:

- Civil Registers of births 1855–2006 (linked to images of full entries, 1855–1908).
- Civil Registers of marriages 1855–2006 (all linked to images, 1855–1933).
- Civil Registers of deaths 1855–2006 (linked to images, 1855–1958).
- Old Parish Registers of births/baptisms, marriages and burials to 1854 (all linked to images).
- Catholic Church records of baptisms, marriages and deaths to 1854 (all linked to images).
- Censuses for 1841, 1851, 1861, 1871, 1881, 1891 and 1901 (all except 1881 linked to images; 1881 links to a transcribed version).

It is possible to search on the following in all of these indexes:

- surname
- forename(s)
- year of registration
- event type (birth/baptism, marriage/banns, death, census)
- sex (male, female, unspecified)
- district

Additional searches in specific indexes:

- Old Parish Register indexes – search on county.
- Old Parish Register births/baptisms – search on parents' names.
- All marriage/banns indexes up to 1932 – search on spouse's name.

- Civil Registers of deaths 1865–1926 and census records – search on age.

It is possible to search for up to five years before and after the year of registration or age typed in, but you will find detailed advice on the ScotlandsPeople website on the best ways to search the database.

Copies of the record entries to which the indexes refer can be ordered online through the website, but at a cost.

As well as being a boon for researchers outside Scotland, the site can also be utilised by more local researchers in preparing a list of references, the full entries for which can then be consulted on a visit to the ScotlandsPeople Centre in Edinburgh, thus making efficient use of time spent there. The site is obviously a very useful resource for those unable to visit Edinburgh, but there remains the difficulty of confidently identifying the correct individual from the information contained in the indexes before obtaining a copy of the full entry. This is where access to the full entries, which is available at no extra charge to those visiting the ScotlandsPeople Centre, is a great advantage, enabling further checking at each step.

1881 BRITISH CENSUS ON CD-ROM

One significant addition to the resources available to the family historian over the last few years has been the 1881 British Census on CD-ROM. This includes about 30 million names on a total of 25 discs. Eight of these store the National Index and sixteen the detailed information transcribed from the census enumerators' schedules. This is divided into eight regions covering Scotland (in two discs), England, Wales, the Isle of Man and the Channel Islands, but not Ireland. The set is completed by a disc containing the family history resource file viewer. Version 2 of the viewer is supplied as standard, but at a small additional cost, you can buy Version 3, which provides additional search options.

The co-operative project which resulted in the production of this set of CD-ROMs was led by the Church of Jesus Christ of Latter-day Saints and permission was granted by the General Register Office for Scotland and the Public Record Office (now the National Archives) for the content of the records in their care to be reproduced in this electronic format.

It is a useful source, not only for family historians, but for other historians too. There are various ways in which the data can be used, but it is our purpose to look specifically at how it might be used for the study of family history.

SEARCHING

The following searches can be made on either the National Index or the regional discs:

- First name
- Last name
- Birth year
- Census place (county or country)

The different additional elements which can be used for searching on each of the two categories of discs are as follows:

- National Index
    Birthplace (county or country).
- Regional discs
    First and middle names
    Birthplace (town or parish).
    By using Neighbours – Advanced Query from the Search menu: any word in Household entries (useful for searches on street names or occupations). An exact phrase search can be done by placing quotation marks around the phrase.

PROBLEMS

The spellings found in the original census records have been followed as closely as possible, so there may be difficulties with variant spellings of names. This has been compensated for to some extent by the use of standardised forms of first and last names. For example, Catherine is the standardised form for Katherine, Kathryn, Kate, and so on, while Hawkins would include spellings such as Haukins and Hockins. A search on any of these variant names would also retrieve the others. There are still some instances when this will not solve the problem, such as people listed with initials rather than full names, like T. Holton, or unusual names that might be spelt differently – Meshec or Meshek.

Ages are often inaccurately recorded in census records, but the search on birth year allows for a range of years up to five years before or after the year you type in, or you could leave this completely blank. Sometimes you may find a family you are searching for but one or more children are missing and this may be because they were living away from home to attend school.

Also, census places may not appear as expected. Uddingston in Lanarkshire is recorded under Bothwell because this was the parish name, although Uddingston and Bothwell were two separate communities.

OTHER WAYS OF SEARCHING

It is possible to browse through the households in the order they were recorded, which could bring up other relatives living nearby and is interesting in giving a picture of the social history of the area at that date.

You can attempt to track down female members of a family who may have married but whose married name is not known. This should be done on the regional discs, where a specific place of birth can be given and is possible if the year of birth is known and if the individual was born in a small parish. The search must be made using the place and year of birth along with the first name of the individual.

You will realise that the production of this set of CD-ROMs has made possible so many ways of searching the data which were quite impossible before. If you are searching for an individual for whom you have only a name, date and place of birth, you now have a good chance of locating them by using the National Index. The CD-ROMs should be available in large libraries, but are very reasonably priced for home users.

1881 CENSUS ON THE WEB

There is a version of the census on the Family Search website (http://www.familysearch.org), but this does not include Scotland. The search options are also more restricted than on the CD-ROM version, as it is not possible to search on street names or occupations.

CASE STUDY

Examples of the kinds of information which can be gleaned from the baptismal and marriage entries in Old Parish Registers are as follows. The examples given here come from the OPRs for North Leith.

Baptismal entry from North Leith OPR

Baptisms in 1824

Ramsay   **John Johnston**, lawful son of **James Ramsay** Fisherman Newhaven & **Margaret Thomson**, was born the 22nd August and Baptized the 2nd September 1824.

Marriage entry from North Leith OPR

Marriages in 1849 – OPR 692(1)/14

Ramsay

&

McDonald

John Ramsay Fisherman Newhaven and Mary-Ann McDonald Newhaven, daughter of James McDonald, Sawyer, Granton gave in their names for proclamation of banns.
Thos. Wilson, Blacksmith, Newhaven
John Affleck, do. , Commercial Str.
Wm. Brown, Elder
Procd. 11 and Married 16 November 1849
Rev. James Fairbairn Minr. Newhaven

From the statutory records of births, marriages and deaths from 1855 onwards and from census information, the examples given here show the types of information and the wealth of detail which can be extracted from such records. It should be clear that all these together can be used to corroborate the information therein, but also conflicts of detail can serve to pose questions in the family historian's enquiring mind. It is important to bear in mind that ages given to census enumerators may have limited accuracy, and that information provided on death certificates concerning the deceased person's parents is more susceptible to error than information on birth and marriage certificates.

1871 census for North Leith

Census for North Leith, 1871 – CEN 1871, 692(1)

No. of Schedule – 170   **Enumeration Book – 16**
 8 James Street, Newhaven

Name	Position	Status	Age	Occupation	Birthplace
John Ramsay	Head	Married	44	Fisherman	Newhaven
Ann Ramsay	Wife	Married	36		Newhaven
James Ramsay	Son	Single	20	Fisherman	Newhaven
John Ramsay	Son	Single	17	Fisherman	Newhaven
Margaret Ramsay	Dau.	Single	13	Scholar	Newhaven
Elisabeth Ramsay	Dau.	Single	9	Scholar	Newhaven

You may have noticed the inaccuracy of the age of the head of the household, compared with the birth date given in the Old Parish Register entry for his baptism in 1824 (an underestimate of two years). It is remarkable to note that both his and his wife's ages were quoted in the 1881 census as only four years older than for the 1871 census.

1881 census for North Leith

Census for North Leith, 1881 – CEN 1881, 692(1)

26 James Street, Newhaven

Name	Position	Status	Age	Occupation	Birthplace
John Ramsay	Head	Married	48	Fisherman	born Newhaven
Maryann Ramsay	Wife		40		born Newhaven
John Ramsay	son		22	Fisherman	born Newhaven
William Ramsay	son		4	scholar	born Newhaven

Information from a death certificate of 1893

Name:	John Ramsay
Occupation:	Fisherman
Status:	Married
When died:	22 September 1893
Where died:	22 Auchinleck's Brae, Newhaven
Age:	about 72 years
Father's name:	James Ramsay (deceased)
Father's occupation:	Fisherman
Mother's name:	Margaret Ramsay (deceased)
Maiden name:	Thomson
Cause of death:	*Morbus Cardis,* Cerebral Embolism
Duration of disease:	10 days
Physician:	Dugald McLaren
Informant's name:	Thos. W. Ramsay
Qualification:	Son
Residence:	
When registered:	22 September 1893
Where:	North Leith
Registrar:	

In the death certificate of 1893, worthy of note, again, is the inaccuracy of the age, but this time it is an overestimate. However, it is important to recognise the quantity of genealogical information provided here:

- Parents' names – this takes us back a full generation, in this case confirming the link mentioned nearly 70 years previously in the baptismal entry of 1824. Details of the father's occupation and the mother's maiden name are provided by the informant. However, be wary, as the informant may not be totally accurate, since it may concern grandparents or people not related to the informant. The fact that they are deceased will allow you to seek prior death certificates for them.
- Informant's name and qualification – in this case it points to the existence of a son not mentioned in available census records.

Information from a death certificate of 1906

Name:	Mary Ann Ramsay
Occupation:	
Status:	Widow of John Ramsay, Fisherman
When died:	4 December 1906, 3.30 a.m.
Where died:	North Poorhouse, Leith
Age:	72 years
Father's name:	James McDonald (deceased)
Father's occupation:	Sawyer
Mother's name:	Margaret McDonald
Maiden name:	Wilson
Cause of death:	Cerebral Haemorrhage
Duration of disease:	2 days
Physician:	G. M. Johnston
Informant's name:	John Burgh
Qualification:	Governor
Residence:	
When registered:	4 December 1906
Where:	Leith
Registrar:	

The death certificate of 1906 provides information concerning the wife of John Ramsay, who is the subject of the death certificate of 1893. In addition to providing details of an earlier generation, this certificate provides possible evidence of either a deterioration in financial circumstances or of her own health with advancing years, requiring her to move to the 'poorhouse' following her husband's death.

CHAPTER 4

SUPPLEMENTARY SOURCES

Now that we have covered the basic, original sources of information for constructing your family history, we take a look at some supplementary sources which you may find to be helpful.

INTERNATIONAL GENEALOGICAL INDEX (IGI)

This massive index is compiled by the Church of Jesus Christ of Latter-day Saints (Mormon Church) and, as far as Scotland is concerned, covers births/baptisms and marriages/banns from the Old Parish Registers and the early years of the Civil Registers. It gives the dates of the events, where registered, the names of the child and father (or both parents if recorded), for births/baptisms, and the names of the bride and groom for marriages/banns. As you will have realised from the earlier descriptions of these records, there may be further useful details included in the originals, and also there can be transcription errors, but nevertheless, the IGI is a very useful and widely used source.

As its name indicates, it covers countries throughout the world and includes several hundred million names. The coverage in England and Wales is less complete than that for Scotland, since the information had to be collected from county record offices/archives and individual parishes, some of which were unwilling to allow the Mormons access to their records. It is now available in several different formats the original microfiche format, Family Search on CD-ROM and as part of the Family Search website. Many reference libraries hold copies of the first and sometimes the second format of the IGI, but the most accessible and easily used version is that on the Web. Here you can search for the names you are looking for, the type of event (birth/christening or marriage), the area (country and county) and the year, up to a range of twenty years before and after the year entered on the screen.

Standardisation of first and last names is used, as in the 1881 British Census on CD-ROM, unless you select the checkbox for Use exact spelling, an option which you must use if you want to include middle names in a search. It is possible to look for children of the same parents, by entering the father's first and last names, the mother's first name and the region. It is also important to remember that nonconformist registers are not included in the index. A small number of deaths and burials are included since some of the information on the Web-based version of the IGI has been contributed by members of the Mormon Church. It is important to be aware of the origins of any record you are looking at in the Index, since, if it is a contributed record, the information should be confirmed from original sources. There should be a clear indication on each record of its origins.

We would emphasise again that the great advantage of this index is its accessibility and it provides a useful source at least for preliminary investigations which can be followed up by more rigorous searching in the original official records.

CURRENT RESEARCH ON THE WEB

With family history now such a widespread interest, it is possibile that another enthusiast may be researching the same family as yourself, so it is worthwhile to investigate this and make contact with any relevant researchers. The most effective way to do this is to search various websites which host family trees contributed by individuals from around the world, check online lists of surnames being researched, search for mailing lists, message boards and forums for the surnames you are interested in, and use search engines to check for websites devoted to particular families. See the List of Websites starting on page 142.

The WorldConnect Project contains family trees submitted by researchers throughout the world and currently includes more than 550 million names. Various forms of trees are used, including pedigree charts showing the ancestors of an individual and descendancy charts showing descendants of an individual. Email links to submitters are also included. This huge collection is well worth searching for names that you are researching. You may come across information about a family you are interested in, and in particular there may be recorded another, hitherto unknown branch of your family, with a link back to one of your own ancestors. There is then the opportunity to try to make contact with the submitter and hopefully exchange data with a new-found relative. A number of websites host collections of family trees to which you can send in your own information if you wish.

To trace whether research is being conducted into the families you are interested in, you should start with the links to various surname lists which can be found on the GENUKI website. These are organised geographically rather than by surname, and provide details of which surnames are being researched in each county. As well as referring to the relevant lists here, you should also make a point of studying the websites of any local family history societies covering the areas you are interested in, since some of these include lists of their members' research interests.

Another area worth investigating, although often tending to have a North American focus, are links to be found on the RootsWeb and GenForum websites.

RootsWeb hosts the RootsWeb Surname List (RSL) of more than one million surnames being researched by family historians throughout the world and also vast numbers of mailing lists devoted to specific surnames. Similar in nature are the surname-based message boards accessible through RootsWeb and the equivalent forums to be found on the GenForum website. All of these have the potential to assist you in discovering whether research is already being carried out on your surnames of interest and by whom.

There are many websites devoted to specific families on the Internet and a search may yield sites relevant to your family names. Remember, however, as with all sites of this nature, including the WorldConnect Project, the information contained may or may not be accurate. It is important to evaluate what you find. Although it may not be completely accurate, important clues to further sources can often be gleaned from this type of information.

For information on how to trace older research on specific families, see the section on local histories and family histories on page 84. There is further information on using the Internet, mailing lists and forums in the following chapter.

FAMILY HISTORY SOCIETIES

There are a large number of family history societies throughout the UK which have been set up with the purpose of promoting family history research, most commonly in a specific geographical area. Meetings are usually held on a regular basis, with guest speakers, and most societies publish their own newsletter. Many now have websites and, as already mentioned, often maintain a register of surnames members are researching, which may be online. In most cases, societies also co-ordinate projects such as the transcription of monumental inscriptions in their own areas.

There are national overseeing bodies for Scotland and England, namely the Scottish Association of Family History Societies and the Federation of Family History Societies. This latter society produces a series of very useful booklets on various aspects of family history.

It is worth joining your local society in order to meet with others who share your hobby. In addition, it can be very worthwhile to join the society covering the area your ancestors lived in. Family history societies have more ready access to some items of particular local interest, and their members, with the benefit of local knowledge, can be very helpful to you in your research. See the list of useful address starting on page 157.

SEARCH STRATEGIES

Here are some suggestions for strategies to follow in your researches, based mainly on the records already described.

- Assemble all the information gathered from your family and your own personal knowledge (as in Chapter 1). The next step is dependent on how far back this information has taken you.

If it has taken you back to 1908 or later:

- Either visit the ScotlandsPeople Centre to search in the statutory registers, or, if not able to visit, apply for copies of birth, marriage and death certificates for the earliest family members for whom you know the year and place of these events. You might find it useful to search the Commonwealth War Graves Commission website if you know of relatives killed in either of the two World Wars but do not know their parents' names (see chapter 5).

If it has taken you to 1907 or earlier:

- Either visit the ScotlandsPeople Centre to search in the statutory registers, census records and Old Parish Registers, or, if not able to visit, search on the ScotlandsPeople website, then apply for copies of relevant records you locate there. You may want to combine these approaches, by preparing a list of references from ScotlandsPeople to be followed up by a visit to the Centre. If you live nearer the registrar's office at Park Circus, Glasgow, or in Dundee, a visit there might be an alternative to visiting Edinburgh.

- Consult the 1881 British Census on CD-ROM if it is easily accessible and you have family details that far back. It would probably be more effective in terms of time and money to search the 1881 Census in this way rather than through the ScotlandsPeople database.

At some point, perhaps when you have reached the middle of the 19th century, it is worthwhile investigating whether other researchers are working on the same family as yourself. As already described, this can be done by checking for family trees online contributed by researchers, through surname lists and members' interests in the local family history societies for the areas you are interested in, and via mailing lists.

CHAPTER 5

FAMILY HISTORY AND THE INTERNET

As the Internet is firmly established as part of everyday life and work, so it has also become an integral part of modern family history research. Family history is one of the most popular subjects on the Internet and vast amounts of genealogical information, both good and bad, can be found there. The benefits are many, but you must also be aware of the drawbacks. The benefits are clear: allowing family members from around the world to communicate easily; making it much easier to discover others who are researching the same families as yourself and then to exchange information with them; the creation of communities of interest, perhaps in one particular surname, a specific geographical area or a topic, with the subsequent benefits which can flow from these types of development; the greatly improved access to information on archives and their holdings and on other genealogy-related organisa-tions, such as local family history societies; and, finally, the opportu-nity to search for and download information from a rapidly increasing number of original sources which can be accessed online.

What, then, are the drawbacks? As we have already suggested, the information available on the Internet is variable in quality. Many sites have been created by family history enthusiasts who have not always based their work on original sources. Assumptions are some-times made about relationships without being backed up by reliable sources. It is important, therefore, to evaluate the information you see. Does it appear to be based on primary sources and, if not, can it be verified for accuracy in these sources?

Although there is now a wealth of wonderful original source mate-rial online, the error rate in many online genealogical indexes is high. Inaccuracies have occurred in the process of transcribing and index-ing as it is often difficult to read original sources. Rigorous checking procedures are required to ensure a high level of accuracy, but often the time and money is not available. In other words, accuracy has been sacrificed on the principle of quantity rather than quality. Of course original sources also include inaccuracies and these, combined with modern transcription and indexing errors, can cause problems at times. It is particularly helpful when links are provided to the digitised version of the original source, to allow data to be verified, but if there are errors in the index, it may be very difficult to locate the original record in the first place. Various techniques can be developed to compensate for these problems, such as searching for other members of a family you are trying to trace in the census records, or searching on just the surname (if not particularly common) and browsing through the results. The practicalities of using techniques such as these vary depending on the nature of the sources you are searching.

WEBSITES

There is a list of useful websites on page 142, but we would like to say a little more about some of these to guide your usage of them.

One of the best resources, to which you can always refer back if you do not know where to go on the Web for help on a genealogical topic, is **Cyndi's List**. This is a highly regarded site with thousands of links relating to all aspects of family history throughout the world. There is one main alphabetical list of categories but it is also possible to search by keyword.

GENUKI is the principal British genealogy site, covering the United Kingdom and Ireland. Here you will find guidance on general topics relating to the whole of this geographical area as well as specific information about smaller areas down to county and sometimes parish level. Lists of family history societies also feature and there are many links to other relevant sites.

ScotlandsPeople gives access to the indexes of births/baptisms in the Old Parish Registers (OPRs) and Catholic records up to 1854 and statutory registers from 1855 to 2006, indexes of banns and marriages in the OPRs and Catholic records up to 1854 and statutory registers from 1855 to 2006, indexes of burials in the OPRs and Catholic records up to 1854, and indexes of deaths in the statutory registers from 1855 to 2006. The images of all the births/baptisms, banns, marriages and burials in the OPR and Catholic records are available, as are those of the entries in the statutory registers of births to 1907, of marriages to 1933 and of deaths to 1957. As far as census records are concerned, indexes to all these from 1841 to 1901 can be searched and the images viewed, except for the 1881 Census, for which transcribed details can be seen. Online payment is required to use this service. This site also gives free access to the index of wills and testaments from 1513 to 1901, with the facility to download images of the documents for a standard charge. Finally there is a free index search of all coats of arms registered in Scotland from 1672 to 1907, with again the opportunity to download images for a standard charge. Some of the entries include text only from the original register, while others also include a colour illustration of the coat of arms. Unfortunately it is not possible to tell from the index entry whether your chargeable download will include text only or text plus an illustration.

FamilySearch is the family history site of the Church of Jesus Christ of Latter-day Saints, including the Web version of the International Genealogical Index as described in Chapter 4. There is, however, much more on the site. Under the Search Records tab, where the IGI is found, there are also the Ancestral File, the Pedigree Resource File and an option to search family history websites. These are all relevant to Scottish research, but there are also other options which include only foreign data.

The Ancestral File is a collection of linked records with pedigree charts and records for family groups which have been submitted to the Church of Latter-day Saints. The Pedigree Resource File is a similar type of database but the records have been submitted by individuals to the FamilySearch Internet Genealogy Service. In the first of these, duplicate records have been merged, which is not the case with the Pedigree Resource File. These databases cover all periods of time up to relatively recently, but do not quote the sources for the data. The Pedigree Resource File can also be purchased on CD-ROM and this version gives details of sources. Because these two databases are compiled from information submitted by individual researchers, the authenticity of the content can vary depending on the accuracy of each researcher. Contact information is given for the contributors of the information.

The family history websites that can be searched from this screen are sites devoted to one or more families which have been notified to the FamilySearch site by users of the site. Again the value of the information on these sites can vary depending on the quality of the research they are based on.

You will notice that it is possible to search all resources from this search screen, but if you choose to select this option, remember that some of the results may not be from original sources and may require verification. As well as the facility to search for individuals, there are other useful sections on the site, including research guidance and research 'helps'. The research guidance section provides guidance suited to the geographical area and period you are researching, while the research 'helps' give descriptions of types of records or how to find particular types of information. You may find it useful to look at these for any assistance they can provide.

The **Commonwealth War Graves Commission** is the organisation responsible for the maintenance of all the cemeteries and war memorials commemorating Commonwealth servicemen and women who were killed during the First and Second World Wars and has a website useful to family historians. Part of the site includes the "Debt of honour register", where all these individuals, as well as Commonwealth civilians killed in the Second World War, are listed. It can be searched by surname and initials and the results of a search gives the rank, service number, date of death, age if known, regiment, nationality and details of the relevant memorial. The use of initials only for Christian names is not very helpful when you are searching for James Campbell or John Macdonald, but the results screen gives fuller names, if available, and you can view details of where the memorial to the individual is located and what the inscription is. Sometimes this gives names of next of kin and so could prove quite informative. The site also includes plans and photographs of the various cemeteries and it is sometimes almost possible to locate an individual's grave on the photographs.

The **Scottish Archive Network (SCAN)** has been set up to provide a single authoritative source of information about the various institutional archives in Scotland. We give fuller details later in this chapter on the SCAN archives catalogue project, and on the wills and testaments project in Chapter 7, but apart from this there is an interesting website. It has various features including a directory with contact information for Scottish archives and associations, with links to their websites where these exist. Another section, Research Tools, includes a glossary, information on Scots currency and weights and measures, and in the Knowledge Base a number of short articles on various topics, people, places and types of record in Scottish history. Linked to from the SCAN website is the Scottish handwriting site, which gives some examples of letter forms and helpful tips on how to read documents.

The **National Archives of Scotland** site gives guidance on the types of record held there and has pages aimed at describing sources useful for family historians. An online catalogue is also available.

The **National Archives**, although based in London, have many records relating to Scots, particularly those who served in the armed forces, since these were administered by the central UK government. The website includes a catalogue of the holdings and a great deal of excellent explanatory material on different types of record and how to use them. The National Archives are also undertaking a large amount of digitisation, so an increasing volume of records is becoming available online, generally with a free index search and the opportunity to download images of the original sources for a standard charge. It is useful to check the website from time to time to identify any new sets or records which have become available online.

RootsWeb.com claims to be the oldest and largest free genealogy site. It includes guidance on how to trace your family tree, the RootsWeb Surname List (RSL) of more than one million surnames being researched by family historians throughout the world, the ROOTS-L mailing list, along with about another 31,000 mailing lists and 161,000 message boards, and links to genealogy projects of various types There are a number of projects in progress which aim to provide free indexes on the Web to important original sources. These are at varying stages of development but are becoming very useful to researchers. Three projects hosted by RootsWeb intend to cover the major original sources used by family historians in the UK: FreeBMD, FreeCEN and FreeREG.

The scope of FreeBMD is limited to England and Wales and is an index to the births, marriages and deaths in the Civil Registers from 1837. The entries give the type of event, name, year and quarter, registration district, volume number, page number and the name of the person who transcribed the data. There is now a vast amount of information included on this database, which is almost complete up to 1929 and totals more than 157 million individual entries.

FreeCEN consists of a searchable database of British census returns for 1841 to 1891, but has not progressed as far as the FreeBMD project. There is a reasonable coverage for Scotland for 1841 and 1851 but little at present for subsequent years.

FreeREG aims to produce an index of baptisms, marriages and burials from UK parish registers and nonconformist registers, but this project is at an early stage and has very little Scottish content so far.

Ancestry.com (and **Ancestry.co.uk**) is a subscription-based service giving access to over 26,000 databases of sources from around the world, which are continually being added to. Ancestry runs a massive digitisation programme covering all types of record of genealogical interest. You will almost certainly find sources of use to you here, but always be well aware of the scope and content of any databases that appear to be relevant before making any financial commitment.

A common practice on sites providing access to original sources is to offer free index searches, with payment required for further content.

It is sometimes possible to gather useful information even from the results of the free searches, but this varies from site to site.

FAMILY HISTORY SOCIETY PROJECTS

Some family history societies are beginning to make data from original sources available via the Internet, one particular example being Aberdeen and North-East Scotland Family History Society, which has compiled an index of over 120,000 names derived from its publications of monumental inscriptions. This can be freely searched on the Internet and gives references to the published lists where the full inscriptions can be found. Check out the websites of any local family history society covering areas you are interested in to see whether similar online sources are available.

ARCHIVE CATALOGUES

One important category of websites are those providing catalogues of archives. Although not giving you online versions of the records themselves, they do help you to locate records which may assist in your researches. Once you move beyond the standard sources described in Chapter 3, it can become difficult to pinpoint the whereabouts of various sources and this is where this type of website becomes so valuable. Previously, and still for the many archives without an online catalogue, the tracking down of these sources usually had to be done by contacting individual archives. Only one local authority archive in Scotland so far has an online catalogue on the Web, Dumfries and Galloway, but the Scottish Archive Network (SCAN) has created a catalogue for almost all of the archives in Scotland. This gives details of the various individual archival collections held by the participating archives and so one search will cover all of these collections. The SCAN online catalogue brings together scattered records about a topic, individual or family and includes the very large collections of the National Archives of Scotland and the manuscripts held by the National Library of Scotland.

There is another possible means of tracing records not held in the National Archives of Scotland, that is, by using the National Register of Archives for Scotland (NRAs) online catalogue and the National Register of Archives (NRA) catalogue. These databases cover material surveyed by the NRAS and NRA, consisting of archival material in Scotland, England, Wales and Ireland, most of which is not held in the national repositories nor in local authority and university archives. These catalogues list records of private individuals, families, businesses and organisations (including churches) which may be located in libraries, museums, offices of organisations and solicitors or in private hands. Although the entries are often very brief, they may be sufficient to lead you to an important source.

The preceding three catalogues are complementary since the SCAN catalogue covers material in the National Archives of Scotland, local authority archives and university archives, while the NRAS and NRA mainly include records held elsewhere.

In England and Wales there are two Web-based archive catalogues which you may wish to consult: the National Archives and A2A. The first of these catalogues the National Archives' holdings which include many records relating to Scottish individuals as referred to later in this book, while A2A provides a catalogue of archives held by over 400 English repositories outwith the National Archives. You might just find some useful leads in these sites, which in some cases give names of individuals mentioned in the documents.

LIBRARIES

There are many publications relating to family history, local history and other topics which you will probably want to consult during the course of your researches, so it is useful to have some knowledge of where to search for these materials.

Very many library catalogues are now on the Web and provide a good resource for checking details and locations of publications. There are useful lists of library catalogues on the Web on the BUBL site, but perhaps the most useful for our purposes are the National Library of Scotland, the Library of Congress in the USA, which has a strong collection of Scottish material, COPAC, which covers many of the major UK university library catalogues as well as the National Library of Scotland and the British Library, the CAIRNS service, which can perform a simultaneous search of almost all of the Scottish university library catalogues and also some public library catalogues, and WorldCat, the largest database of published (and some unpublished) material held in libraries throughout the World. The useful Bibliography of Scotland is on the National Library of Scotland's website (coverage from 1988). Should you find that a title of interest is held by a library far from your own home, it may be possible to obtain it through the Inter-Library Loan service, details about which are available from your local library. Some libraries also have extensive collections of manuscripts, particularly university libraries and the National Library of Scotland, and information about these, including catalogues, is gradually appearing on the Web.

MAILING LISTS

Mailing lists on the Internet consist of a group of people, small or very large in number, who subscribe (free of charge) to the list. They can then send a message on a topic relevant to the interests of that list. The message is circulated to all the subscribers either singly or as a digest compiled from the messages of a number of members. Depending on the number of members in the mailing list and how active they are, there may be only occasional messages or, on the other hand there may be one or two digests every day.

There are now numerous genealogy mailing lists in existence, in fact thousands, and these can be a good way of making contacts and of asking specific questions about research methods, sources and individuals or families. Often members of these lists will do 'lookups' for other members, by checking for a particular name in a source to which they have access.

Some genealogy mailing lists, such as GENBRIT, are concerned with research in a particular geographical area, in this case England, Wales and Scotland. Many counties also have their own specialist lists. Other lists are devoted to the study of a particular surname (as we have already seen in Chapter 4) or to a topic such as medieval genealogy, royal genealogy, or computers and family history. The best way to find out about mailing lists is to consult Cyndi's List or RootsWeb, which hosts the vast majority of these lists. It is probably a good plan to join one or two lists which, apart from any other advantages, can help to keep you up to date with developments in particular fields of family history.

FORUMS

Similar to mailing lists are the many message boards or forums. The RootsWeb site has more than 161,000 message boards, while GenForum hosts many thousands. These are discussion forums on individual surnames, geographical areas or topics, to which messages can be posted asking questions and providing information. While mailing lists automatically send to all the subscribers e-mails containing messages sent to the list, forums are viewed on the Web with messages grouped into discussions on particular topics.

The **MyFamily.com** website is an Internet community for families that uses password control to ensure a safe environment. Families can use it to keep in touch using chats and can create family albums and calendars of events and update family trees.

ONLINE FAMILY HISTORY COURSES

There are online courses on family history, some freely accessible, and other, more extensive courses, requiring payment. Some of the latter can lead to the award of postgraduate certificates and diplomas. The Federation of Family History Societies website provides links to information about various online courses available in Britain, while Cyndi's List gives links to information on courses based in Canada and the USA, which generally contain material relevant to research in Britain as well as in their home countries.

CASE STUDIES

A few examples may suffice to give you some idea of the results that can be achieved using various websites currently available.

In researching the Crawfurd family of Jordanhill, the use of the National Register of Archives site revealed the fact that a collection of manuscripts relating to the family was held by the National Library of Scotland. The collection was examined, copies were ordered of some of the material and a family tree was compiled using the information. In order to supplement what had already been found, it seemed worth checking the WorldConnect Project for any information submitted by others researching the same family. Sure enough, a good deal of material was available, bringing down some lines of descent to the present day, and subsequently contact was made by e-mail with the descendant who had submitted the information. This opened up the possibility of an exchange of any relevant material.

Mailing lists tend to include many messages notifying the list of members' research interests in the hope that other members may have the same interests and be able to come up with more useful information. The Suffolk mailing list was notified of an interest in a specific Hicks family, leading to an exchange of information. Along with contacts made through the Timperley of Hintlesham website, this resulted in an informal group coming together and corresponding by e-mail on family history matters.

An example taken from one branch of this Hicks family serves to illustrate how information can be gleaned from the Commonwealth

War Graves Commission site. C. H. Hicks was killed in the First World War and by searching in the Commission's 'Debt of honour register' under Hicks, C., selecting First World War and nationality United Kingdom, we find thirteen names listed. It is now a fairly easy task to identify the correct individual. The details provided are quite informative, giving his parents' names and his place of birth. Many entries do not contain as much information, but you may be lucky enough to find an important extra piece of data there.

A final example relates again to the WorldConnect Project. Some time ago a reference had been noticed to the possibility of a relationship between the Howard Dukes of Norfolk and William Shakespeare, quoting the relevant surnames as Moleyns, Whalesborough and Arden. Having spent a little time researching some published material on the ancestry of Shakespeare, information was found about Shakespeare's mother, Mary Arden, and her family and it was known that John Howard, 1st Duke of Norfolk had certainly been married to Katherine Moleyns. Otherwise there was no obvious link and this particular line of research was dropped for a time. Revisiting the problem later, the WorldConnect Project was searched for any clues and there certainly were some. By searching for Whalesborough and then browsing through the descendants, links were found to Katherine Moleyns, whose mother was a Whalesborough, and to Eleanor Hampden (whose mother was also a Whalesborough), wife of Walter Arden. This pointed to where further research was needed and although a connection between the Howards and Shakespeare was not finally proved, the research had been moved on another stage with the help of the Web. In addition, it revealed the link with the Hampden family from whom the famous seventeenth century parliamentarian John Hampden was descended. This led on to contact with the John Hampden Society via its website and e-mail, which may eventually result in some of the Hampden family history being made available on the site.

We hope that at least some of these examples have given you an insight into practical ways in which the Web can help you with your research. Try it out; you never know what you might find.

CHAPTER 6

HISTORICAL INFORMATION

So far we have looked only at what could be described as 'genealogical sources', giving details of births, baptisms, marriages, deaths and burials. These record major events in individuals' lives and provide family links. They give us the basic facts from which we can construct a family tree. Of course, these sources sometimes also give us a bit extra, such as the occupations and residences of our relatives, but for our purposes they are important for the genealogical information. If you want to build up a real family history, rather than just a genealogy, you will need to move on to researching in what we will describe as 'historical sources'. These record details of individuals' lives through dates, places and activities which are additional to the major 'life events' covered by the 'genealogical sources' and are very varied.

'THE REAL THING': PRIMARY SOURCES

Primary, or original sources compiled at the period of time being studied, are the basis of all research and fall into several categories, so firstly we will have a look at various listings, which tend to cover a wider range of the population than other sources.

LISTINGS

Valuation rolls, 1855–
These rolls were compiled as lists of those liable to pay tax on the value of their property (rates) and are arranged by the address of the property concerned. From 1855 onwards there are annual rolls for each burgh and county, listing properties with the names and designations of the proprietor, tenant and occupier and its value. Unfortunately, occupiers of property at a rental of less than £4 a year did not have to be named and only the heads of households were included.

These records, a complete set of which is available in the National Archives of Scotland, can be difficult to search, being arranged by address rather than by individuals' names. This means that if you are searching for a family in a large town, but do not have an address, you will probably have to hunt laboriously through several volumes which may be oddly arranged and whose arrangement may change from year to year. Sometimes the names of streets changed over a period of years and also the street numbers. Should you happen to be interested in Edinburgh or Glasgow, you will encounter extra problems, although there is a source of valuation records for Glasgow which may provide some consolation. The valuation rolls for these two cities are divided up by parishes, up to 1895 in Edinburgh and 1909 in Glasgow, and after these dates, by wards. In order to track down the street you are looking for, you could consult large-scale Ordnance Survey maps of the period, street directories, which show the ward numbers of streets, or, for Glasgow, the 1875–6 index of streets, giving the parishes for each street. After 1912, the valuation rolls for Edinburgh have street indexes. The Glasgow and Edinburgh street indexes are to be found in the National Archives of Scotland. Otherwise, those materials for tracking down a specific street relating to Edinburgh can be found in Edinburgh Central Library and those for Glasgow in the Mitchell Library there. Some valuation rolls can be found in local reference libraries or archives, but usually only relate to the period after about 1880.

The other source for Glasgow is the Valuation Roll Index, covering the rolls for 1832, 1861, 1881 and 1911. Available in the Glasgow City Archives, this computerised database arose out of a project on housing patterns in Glasgow from 1832 to 1911 conducted by the University of Strathclyde and contains the names of 352,486 individuals who were proprietors or occupiers in Glasgow during this period. Along with the names, it gives their occupations and addresses and is searched by names. There is also a reference number given, but the rolls themselves for this period are not held in the Glasgow City Archives.

The valuation rolls are one of several record sets undergoing digitisation and should become accessible online over the next year. A few earlier valuation rolls do exist and these are described in Chapter 7.

A similar set of records, held in the National Archives of Scotland, are those of the Inland Revenue Valuation Office and include a survey of every property in Scotland in 1911 and 1912. This gives the names of owners, tenants and occupiers along with valuation details and there are associated maps with the properties marked.

Electoral registers

Also useful are the electoral registers, although they have not survived as well as the valuation rolls. Before the Reform Act of 1832 was passed, only a very small percentage of the population was entitled to vote, but from 1832 onwards, this percentage increased with the passing of several other Reform Acts. Details of who was allowed to vote can be found in *Electoral registers since 1832* by Jeremy Gibson. Very briefly, from 1832 to 1867 electors in parliamentary elections were male proprietors or tenants of lands or houses. In 1868 the category of male lodgers paying an annual rent of at least £10 was added. Women, although not receiving the vote in parliamentary elections until 1918, were given the vote in burgh council and county council elections from 1882 and 1889 respectively if they were proprietors or tenants. These women voters are recorded in separate registers for local government elections. Obviously, until 1918 there was a considerable proportion of the population who still could not vote, since from 1910 to 1918 the electorate in Scotland almost trebled. For most of the period, in the cities, the names are arranged by electoral wards. Despite this, you may still be able to pinpoint the address of relatives at a particular date, which could in turn help you to locate them in the census returns. The information provided for the period 1832–1918 is the name, occupation, whether a proprietor, tenant or prosperous lodger and the property which qualified the elector to vote. It should be remembered that the elector may not have been living at the address of the property which entitled him to vote.

The Registers which have survived are scattered, some in the National Archives of Scotland, particularly those between 1832 and the 1870s and others in local archives and libraries. The Mitchell Library has a continuous set for Glasgow from 1846 appearing annually, except for periods during the two World Wars. There are separate registers for the burghs and counties. In many cases, a constituency consisted of several burghs perhaps in more than one county, while the registers for the counties are listed by parish. There are also some registers for the burghs among the sheriff court records and other odd registers in some Gifts and Deposits collections of the National Archives of Scotland.

Street and trade directories

Other listings that can prove very helpful are street and trade directories, which are available mainly for the large cities. There are long runs of Post Office directories for Edinburgh (annual from 1805) and Glasgow (annual from 1803), with a few other directories dating back to 1783 in Glasgow and 1773 in Edinburgh. Once again the coverage is quite limited, particularly in the early years, and tends to include the notable and well off members of society, those with their own business or trade and those in official positions. Often these directories consist of three listings, one alphabetically by surname, one street by street and another for trades and businesses. Businessmen may be listed under both a business and home address or they may own several shops, each being mentioned individually. Although mainly useful for researching the cities, there were a few directories published covering the Scottish counties, such as Pigot's directories for 1820, 1825 and 1837 and Slater's directory, which appeared in twenty editions between 1852 and 1928.

These directories can be found in large reference libraries or in local libraries in the area the directory covers. The Glasgow directories from 1801 to 1886 are also available on microfiche, while you can find the Glasgow directory for 1787 at two addresses on the Web. The first of these websites also includes the entries for Ayrshire towns in Pigot's directory for 1837.

As an example, here is the entry for John McPhail, who, due to his position as a mail-coach guard, merited inclusion in the Glasgow directories from 1801 to 1805:

M'Phail, J. Greenock mail-coach guard, Old Wynd

You might also be able to use street directories to trace a private resident over a number of years and if they have been listed regularly and are of a good age, their disappearance from the directory can be a clue that they have died. Other sources can then be used to confirm this or otherwise. Two unmarried Holton sisters lived together in Uxbridge Road, London, for many years in the early part of the twentieth century. By this date, a good number of private residents were being included in the street directories in addition to the notables, business and tradespeople and those in the professions. As a result, the Holton sisters could be traced year after year at the same address, until the death of Laura Elizabeth Holton in 1919. Another reason why a name which had been regularly included in a directory should then disappear could be interpreted as a move out of the area, particularly if the person was not elderly.

Church members
There are quite a number of lists of church members from the nineteenth century or earlier in the National Archives of Scotland.

Some of these are separate lists, entitled 'list of communicants', 'communion roll' or something similar, and included only adults, but visitation lists, examination rolls or catechismal rolls also list children. These were used by the local ministers to ensure that those over a certain age knew the catechism. A record of younger children was kept for future reference. Other similar lists are included in some kirk session minutes. Sometimes these give information about parishioners who had moved from another parish and the date they joined the church. It might also be worth checking whether the church had an account book listing those who rented seats in the church, a practice which was quite common at one time. These lists exist for both the Church of Scotland and other churches and local archives also hold this type of material.

POOR LAW RECORDS

Although 1845 saw the passing of the Poor Law (Scotland) Act, this did not bring about a major change either in those entitled to help or in those running the system. Normally, only the poor who were over the age of 70, those unable to work due to disability or insanity, or children who had been orphaned or were destitute were eligible for poor relief. The unemployed who were fit to work received no help for themselves, but their children might qualify. Basic responsibility for assisting the poor lay with the parish in which they were born or had lived for a specified period of time.

Parochial boards were set up after the 1845 Act to run the system, but in practice, most of their members were the same people who had managed poor relief before 1845. As a result, the records often appear in kirk session records or heritors records, kept in the National Archives of Scotland. (The heritors were the landowners of the parish.) Where separate records exist for the parochial boards and their successors, from 1894 the parish councils, these are found among county council, district council and burgh records, stored mainly in local archives. A small number are kept in the National Archives of Scotland.

The information provided in the poor relief records from 1845 is certainly better than for the earlier period, giving the age, place of birth and the name and age of the pauper's spouse and children, whether they were living in the same residence or not.

There were applicants who were not successful and often they are mentioned in parochial board minutes, or in a separate list. Should they have made an appeal against the decision, their case would be recorded in the sheriff court records in the National Archives of Scotland.

Particular to the Highlands and Islands were the destitution boards created in 1846 to provide money, meal or work for those affected by the failure of the potato crop. Their records cover the years 1847 to 1852 and are also in the National Archives of Scotland.

There are now several computerised indexes of Poor Law records available, the largest being for Glasgow, which is maintained in Glasgow City Archives. This covers the period from 1851 to 1910, with over 300,000 entries, and can be searched by personal names. It can be particularly useful in tracing birthplaces of many poor Irish who flooded into Glasgow in the middle of the last century and is very easy to use.

Glasgow City Archives also have two other similar computerised indexes, one for Lanarkshire, covering the period up to 1900, and another for Dunbartonshire, Renfrewshire and Bute, again covering up to 1900. There is also an Ayrshire Poor Relief Database freely available online, which covers a number of parishes from the middle of the nineteenth century. One of the parishes covered is Ardrossan, whose records are a good source for information on Irish immigrants.

An example of a different approach is that taken by the Troon and Ayrshire Family History Society, which is putting a fairly complete version of the Register of Poor Relief Applications for Dreghorn on the Web. At present this covers 1872 to 1879 and 1886 to 1890, but is not indexed. Each time period of one or two years can be searched using the 'Find' feature on your Web browser.

OCCUPATIONAL RECORDS

Coal miners

Being one of the main Scottish industries during the nineteenth and the first half of the twentieth century, mining was a major employer, so there is a fair chance that one of your relatives may have been a miner.

The records in which you may trace some information are those of the National Coal Board. These records, also in the National Archives of Scotland, include the records of coal mining companies from before nationalisation in 1947 which date back in some cases to the eighteenth century. Most, however, are twentieth century and the details usually just consist of the names of miners with the work they had done and what they were paid.

At one time, many landowners ran mines on their estates and

their records may be in the Gifts and Deposits collections in the National Archives of Scotland.

Railwaymen

Most of the surviving records of the many railway companies which used to exist in Scotland are kept in the National Archives of Scotland. Some of the records of staff give the employee's date of birth and details of the various posts held while working for the company. The best collection of staff records is that of the North British Railway Company and there are also some railway records in the Gifts and Deposits collections.

To utilise these sources you will need to have an idea of which company your relative worked for. Helpful for this purpose is *British railways pre-grouping atlas and gazetteer*, which gives information about the companies before 1923.

For a more detailed survey of this subject, have a look at *Was your grandfather a railwayman?* (Richards 2002).

Armed forces

Since the Army and Navy were run from London, almost all the records are held in the National Archives there. For detailed information about the many manuscript sources which are held there you should check the National Archives website or *Tracing your ancestors in the National Archives* (Bevan 2006).

Due to the fact that these records are kept outwith Scotland, you may find it particularly useful to try tracing your relative in printed sources available in large reference libraries.

Royal Navy

As far as the Navy is concerned, the printed sources only include officers, so are of limited use. 'Steel's Navy List' 1782–1817, the annual 'Navy List' 1814– and 'The New Navy List', 1839–1855, cover this period, but the *Naval biographical dictionary* by W. R. O'Byrne, published in 1849, gives more information for all the officers ranked lieutenant and above who were active or retired in 1846. The father of the officer is often listed, making this a very useful source.

As already mentioned, there are many sources available in the National Archives, but as you can imagine, it is much easier to trace an officer than a rating. One of the main sources which lists all the officers and ratings on board a particular ship is the series of ships' musters held in the National Archives covering Scotland from 1707 to 1878. These give the place of birth and usually the age of ratings, but the big disadvantage is that you must know the name of the ship on which your relative served. Fortunately, from 1853, you can trace any naval seaman by name only, in the Continuous Service Engagement Books 1853–1872 and the Registers of Seamen's Services 1873–1895. Here you will find the date and place of birth and details of his service.

Army

Once again, the main printed source, 'The Army List', first issued in 1740 and then annually from 1754, only gives officers and there are manuscript lists of officers for 1707 to 1752 in the National Archives at Kew. Most important amongst the manuscript sources for other ranks are the muster books and pay lists, the main series beginning in 1732. You will need to know the regiment your relative served in to use these records, but if you manage to trace him back to the date of enlistment, you should find his age and the place he enlisted, although not always his place of birth. Another useful series of records are the 'Soldiers' Documents' 1760–1913, which give details of soldiers who were discharged to pension. These are arranged by regiment (to 1872), then in four categories (to 1883) and finally the arrangement is alphabetical by surname. The information given relates to the soldiers' army service as well as his age, place of birth and previous occupation. After 1883, some additional details of family are listed. These sources are all housed in the National Archives.

There are some details of militia amongst the sheriff court and county council records and in some Gifts and Deposits collections in the National Archives of Scotland and also housed there are some Ministry of Defence records with lists of members of territorial and auxiliary forces associations. Information on volunteer forces can also be found in some of the Gifts and Deposits collections.

Royal Air Force

Records up until the mid-1920s of those serving in the RAF, formed in 1918, and its predecessors, the Royal Flying Corps and Royal Naval Air Service, are available in the National Archives. Further details can be found on their website, while 'The Air Force List', published from 1919, lists RAF personnel.

A number of online databases exist with information on those who served in the armed forces, including the Medal Rolls Index, listing virtually all soldiers and airmen who served in the First World War, their pension records and service records (only about

25 per cent of the service records have survived), soldiers who died in the Great War 1914–1919, and Royal Navy service records of those who joined as ratings, 1853–1923. These databases allow a free index search, with payment required to download further information.

Many local newspapers published Rolls of Honour of those killed in the World Wars, often including photographs. One particularly important example was the *Evening Times* Roll of Honour, printed during the First World War, by the Glasgow-based newspaper, but not confined to Glasgow citizens. An index to this is being placed online, already with about 10,000 names, and work is still ongoing.

Merchant seamen

The main sources of information on merchant seamen in this period are agreements made between the masters of ships and crew members before they set sail. Such agreements became compulsory in 1835 and as a result there are various crew lists in the National Archives of Scotland, Glasgow City Archives, the National Archives, the National Maritime Museum in London and the Memorial University, Newfoundland. The agreements quote the name, age and place of birth of the crew members, but unless you know the name of the ship to search, or in some cases the port, it will be like looking for a needle in a haystack, or perhaps a fish in the ocean.

Rather more accessible is the online database of Second World War medals issued to merchant seamen, 1946–2002. Once again there is a free index search, with payment required to download further information.

Businesses

Many records of businesses have now found their way to archives and in some cases these include records giving employees' names, especially wages books. To see what is available, you will need to check with the National Archives of Scotland, the National Register of Archives for Scotland, the Business Records Centre at the Glasgow University Archives, and local archives. The Business Records Centre has a particularly good collection of material for the West of Scotland, while the Scottish Brewing Archive, also held in the Glasgow University Archives, includes records of many companies from the Edinburgh area. One other source available in the Glasgow University Archives is a computer index of bankruptcies for the period from about 1745 to 1914. This index is also available in the National Archives of Scotland, where the original records concerning bankruptcies are held.

If you are looking for information about either the Bank of Scotland and its constituent banks from 1695 or the Royal Bank of Scotland, you should note that they both have their own archives. The Royal Bank's website has an archive guide giving details of the records held from the 1660s onwards. Both of these archives include not only the records of the various banks, but also some business collections.

Clergymen

Information on clergymen from most of the main denominations can be found in printed sources, the most important being the *Fasti Ecclesiae Scoticanae*. This consists of several volumes detailing the ministers of the Church of Scotland from 1560 onwards and gives biographical and family information about them. Most of this can be freely accessed online.

Other publications are listed in the Bibliography. You may wish to look for additional information by consulting the records of the churches themselves or contacting the offices of the relevant denomination.

School teachers

Many books have been written about individual schools in Scotland and so you might find it worthwhile to begin any search for relatives who were school teachers by investigating whether anything has been written about the school or area which interests you. Very useful here are *A bibliography of Scottish education before 1872* (1970) and *A bibliography of Scottish education 1872–1972* (1974), both by James Craigie. These list both books and articles and if there is any material on your school or area, the chances are it will be mentioned.

Moving on to manuscript sources, which are in the National Archives of Scotland or local archives, we find a change in responsibility for schools occurring in 1872 when education became compulsory in Scotland, with the passing of the Education (Scotland) Act. Before this time, teachers in the burghs were appointed by the burgh council and are recorded in the council minutes. Outwith the burghs, the normal procedure was for the heritors and minister of each parish to nominate a schoolmaster who was interviewed by the presbytery to establish his suitability. Appointments of parish schoolmasters were mentioned in the heritors records with the confirmation by the presbytery in the presbytery minute books. Since the schoolmaster often became the session clerk, he may also be mentioned in the Kirk Session records.

The formation of the Free Church of Scotland in 1843 also resulted in the founding of Free Church schools whose teachers were appointed by the deacons of the Church. The deacons' court minutes is the source which records these appointments.

The problems of the lack of schools in the Highlands and Islands attracted special attention from three sources, the Government, the Society in Scotland for Propagating Christian Knowledge (SSPCK) and a Mr James Dick.

There are records of grants made by the Government to finance extra schools in these areas for the period 1840 to 1863 and these name the schoolmasters receiving them.

The SSPCK also set up schools in the Highlands and Islands and an alphabetical list of the schoolmasters, with their dates of service, can be found in *SSPCK schoolmasters 1709–1872*, edited by A. S. Cowper (1997).

Finally we turn to Mr James Dick. In accordance with his will, the Dick Bequest Trust was set up to provide assistance to schoolmasters in country parishes in the counties of Aberdeen, Banff and Moray. The Trust's records begin in 1832 and may prove useful if you had a teacher relative working in that area. These records and those relating to Government grants are held in the National Archives of Scotland.

A printed annual calendar of certificated teachers was produced in the period 1850 to 1857, giving names of teachers and the schools or colleges they were associated with. This is not readily available, but was issued as part of the Committee of Council on Education minutes and then separately for 1857–8. There is a set held in Jordanhill Library, University of Strathclyde.

The Educational Institute of Scotland was founded in 1847 as a professional association for teachers, and its records, which are deposited in the National Archives of Scotland, give the names of its members. Within this collection are some earlier records of societies for teachers in Glasgow (1794–1836), Roxburgh (1811–1840) and Jedburgh (1824–1872).

In 1872 the responsibility for the provision of schools passed to school boards, which mentioned the appointment of teachers and pupil-teachers in their minute books. These usually formed part of the county council records and may be kept in local archives or libraries, although a few are in the National Archives of Scotland.

Other sources are detailed in *Tracing your Scottish ancestors: The official guide* (National Archives of Scotland 2009), but these tend to cover short periods or only a small number of schools.

Doctors

A considerable amount of information is available about doctors from published sources, namely the 'Medical Register', published annually from 1859 and the 'Medical Directory'. The 'Medical Directory' appeared under that title from 1870 onwards, but before this, Scottish doctors are listed in the 'Medical Directory for Scotland' 1852–1860 and then the 'London and Provincial Medical Directory' 1861–1869. This is also an annual and gives more details than the 'Medical Register'. There is often a brief summary of the individual's career, with qualifications, positions held and perhaps references to any published work they had produced.

If you are trying to trace a doctor from before 1858, it may be worth contacting one or more of the three professional bodies concerned with the profession, the Royal College of Surgeons of Edinburgh, the Royal College of Physicians and Surgeons of Glasgow, or the Royal College of Physicians of Edinburgh. The first two of these bodies could license surgeons and doctors to practise and have records of licentiates dating back to 1770 and 1785 respectively. In the case of the Royal College of Physicians of Edinburgh, the procedure was different and their licentiates would all have studied at a university. It should be said that these lists of licentiates include little information and the university records could be a more fruitful source for those doctors and surgeons who studied there.

Other medical and related professions

Registers of nurses from 1885 to 1930 are preserved in the National Archives of Scotland and then from 1921 there were registers published annually. Midwives, dentists and chemists can also be sought in published annual registers from 1917, 1879 and 1869 respectively, although these published registers are not easily accessible.

Another avenue for tracing medical workers, particularly those associated with hospitals, are the records of health boards, many of which begin in the eighteenth century. Of course these also include a good deal of information about patients, but being un-indexed, could prove very difficult to use for this purpose. Major collections are preserved for Dumfries and Galloway Health Board at Crichton Royal Hospital, Dumfries, for Northern Health Services at Aberdeen Royal Infirmary, for NHS Greater Glasgow and Clyde Board at Glasgow University Archives, and for Lothian Health Services at

Edinburgh University Library. Both the last two have websites containing catalogues of their collections, which, as well as the expected hospital records, include gifts and deposits of papers from individuals connected in some way with the medical professions.

Lawyers

Once again, printed sources will probably be the first port of call in the search for relatives in the legal profession. If your relative was an advocate, which meant he could plead cases in the Court of Session, he should appear in *The Faculty of Advocates, 1532–1943* (Scottish Record Society). Here you will normally find the name of the advocate's father, the date of his own birth and death and details of any marriages. Solicitors, or, as they used to be called, writers, should be listed in *The register of the Society of Writers to the Signet* (1983), covering the period from the fifteenth century to the 1980s, although this is not comprehensive. *The history of the Society of Writers to her Majesty's Signet* (1890) also contains a list of members from 1594 to 1890 and is online. Many Aberdeen solicitors are listed in the *History of the Society of Advocates in Aberdeen* (Henderson 1912), which is also online.

The main annual published list of lawyers is the *Scottish law list* published for 1848–49 and then the *Index juridicus: The Scottish law list* from 1852 onwards.

There are various manuscript records in the National Archives of Scotland, but you will probably not need to resort to them for this period. Details can be found in *Tracing your Scottish ancestors: the official guide*.

EDUCATIONAL SOURCES

School pupils

A small number of schools have published lists of pupils and you may be able to trace these in local libraries. Many admission registers have survived and also school log books, recording the day-to-day events in the schools. These log books do mention names of pupils, but apart from this, they can provide some anecdotal background information for your family history. These school records tend to date from 1872, but some are earlier and you will normally find them in local archives. Otherwise, there are leaving-certificate registers from 1908 in the National Archives of Scotland, listing all those presented for the leaving certificate. However, there is a 75-year closure period on these.

University students

All of the four oldest Scottish universities have published information about their former students, some much more extensively than others.

Glasgow has published matriculation albums for 1728 to 1858 and the roll of graduates, 1727 to 1897. The first of these works gives fuller information than the second, usually listing the name of the graduate's father and other biographical details. The university alumni website gives details of Glasgow University graduates from 1451 to 1896.

There are published registers for St Andrews covering 1413 to 1588 and 1747 to 1897 and for Aberdeen, covering 1495 to 1955, some of which are online.

Finally, Edinburgh has only published lists of graduates in particular subjects, although the earliest register of graduates, for 1587 to 1809, is online.

Consult the Bibliography for fuller details of these and the List of Websites for some which are available online.

Some of the registers provide little more than a list of names, but it may be worthwhile contacting the university itself, to check whether it has some unpublished records.

An example from the Glasgow University Matriculation Albums illustrates the type of information you may find:

1834 A.D. 13232 RICARDUS SHAEN *filius natu secundus Samuelis jurisconsulti in parochia de Hatfield Peverell et comitatu de Essex.* Born in 1817. BA 1836, MA 1837. Minister at (1) Lancaster, 1842–5, (2) Edinburgh, 1845–50, (3) Dudley, 1852–5, (4) Royston, Herts, 1855–94. Died 24 January 1894.

Other useful online resources, relating to university students and graduates, are the World War I and World War II Rolls of Honour of Glasgow University. These list individuals associated with the university who were killed in the wars and in some cases include a photograph and other biographical details.

Students of other educational institutions

A number of Scottish colleges were founded in the nineteenth century and records of students have often survived. For example, Jordanhill College of Education, now the Faculty of Education of the University of Strathclyde, has student registers from the middle of the nineteenth century, as well as various other sources such as letter books which often mention students. National registers of candidates qualifying as teachers at the various teacher training colleges were published annually from 1857 to 1907 and an almost complete set is held in Jordanhill Library, University of Strathclyde.

You should contact the particular college itself to confirm whether any relevant documents have survived and if so, where they are kept.

An additional aid to assist the tracing of records of higher education institutions is now available in the form of the Archives Hub, a web-based catalogue of archives held by many of these institutions throughout the United Kingdom.

NEWSPAPERS

Although these can be a very useful and illuminating source, particularly for filling in interesting details about individuals, they are often very difficult to use, given that most are un-indexed. This means some very laborious searching, especially for the most interesting news items. There are also the notices of births, marriages and deaths, and obituaries for well-known characters from the area, which are fairly easy to locate in each issue of the paper, but to pick up news stories, your task is much more difficult. The *Glasgow Herald* has an index for the period 1906 to 1984 and recently a number of projects have been set up to index local newspapers, but the proportion covered is very small.

To trace whether there are any newspapers covering the area and period you are interested in, consult the *Directory of Scottish newspapers*, compiled by Joan P. S. Ferguson, which also lists where copies can be found.

THE 'REAL THING', ONCE REMOVED: SECONDARY SOURCES

LOCAL HISTORIES AND FAMILY HISTORIES

Although the original, or primary, sources are the basis of all research, secondary sources such as local and family histories are worth consulting, not only for the possibility of finding specific information about your family, but also to gather background historical information relating to a particular locality or family. Usually you will find a good collection of such works in the local library or in the main reference libraries such as Edinburgh City Library or the

Mitchell Library in Glasgow. To investigate whether any histories have been published about the area or family you are researching, consult for local histories *A contribution to the bibliography of Scottish topography* (Mitchell and Cash 1917), *A bibliography of works relating to Scotland 1916–1950* (Hancock 1959) and the *Bibliography of Scotland* produced by the National Library of Scotland, covering the period 1976 onwards (from 1988 onwards available on the National Library website); and for family histories, *Scottish family histories* (Ferguson 1986).

BIOGRAPHICAL REFERENCE SOURCES

You might think it unlikely that any members of your family would appear in dictionaries of biography, but since these are fairly accessible in reference libraries and because as your research progresses you may discover new family names and people of some importance, it is worth looking.

The main reference work of British biographies is the *Oxford dictionary of national biography*. This is the successor to the original *Dictionary of national biography* (DNB) and is also available online through some library services. It contains biographies of individuals arranged alphabetically, but obviously many other names are briefly mentioned and in the online version it is possible to search for these.

The British biographical archive, published by Bowker-Saur on microfiche in two series includes entries from several hundred reference works published in the period 1601 to 1974, but not including the original DNB or *Who was who*. It is only likely to be available in very large reference libraries.

The volumes of *Who was who* are compiled from *Who's who* and include many who have not gained an entry in the *Oxford dictionary of national biography*. These cover from 1897 onwards, with an index volume covering 1897 to 1990. The annual volumes of *Who's who* itself begin in 1849, although prior to 1897 they are little more than lists of names. There is also an online version for 1898 to the present day, available by subscription.

Another work of possible use is *Modern English biography*, by Frederic Boase, first published between 1892–1921, which, despite its title, includes many Scots. This work, in six volumes, provides brief biographies of persons who died between 1851 and 1900.

Specifically Scottish biographies are covered by *The biographical dictionary of eminent Scotsmen* (Chambers 1835) and *The Scottish nation* (Anderson 1880), but only fairly major figures are included. *The Scottish nation* includes information on surnames and families as well as on individuals. There is also the recent *Scottish biographical dictionary*, but again this only covers the most famous.

If you think you have a connection to the nobility or landed gentry, you should consult *Burke's peerage*, *Burke's landed gentry*, *Debrett's peerage* and in particular, for Scotland, *The Scots peerage* by Sir James Balfour Paul. There are also a number of biographical dictionaries dealing with important figures associated with a particular area, such as *Who's who in Glasgow in 1909*, or connected with a subject such as science or music, for example *British musical biography*, published in 1897.

CASE STUDY

Here is a real example of how some of the sources mentioned in this Chapter can be used to research a family's history.

Margaret Conway was left a widow at the end of December 1879, with the unexpected death of her husband James at the age of 39. Having five young children aged 10 down to 1, she was in need of assistance and so applied for poor relief in 1880. This is recorded in the Poor Relief Applications database in Glasgow City Archives in which married women are indexed under both their married and maiden surnames. The original record provides very useful information, giving the age and birthplace of the applicant and the names and ages of her children. Also, to establish responsibility for financial assistance to be given, the addresses at which the family had lived over the previous few years are listed. Finally, and what could be most useful to a researcher, the age of the dead husband is given along with his place of birth, which was Greyabbey in Ireland. This last piece of information could be very difficult to discover in any other way and so provides a very helpful pointer for further research on James Conway and his family. The details of the family's addresses also shows how they moved very frequently over this period of time and gives us a small insight into one aspect of their lifestyle.

Moving back in time, we know from the marriage certificate of James Conway and Margaret Gray of 1866 that Margaret was living at 33 Green Street at that time and that her parents were Hugh Gray (deceased) and Margaret Gray, maiden surname Dougall. It would be helpful to gather as much information about the family before passing the 'threshold' of 1855 into the period of parish registers and the best source for this would be the census of 1861. By using the Valuation Rolls database in Glasgow City Archives it might be possible to check very quickly the address in 1861 of her parents, or mother, if Hugh Gray was dead by this date. Sure enough, Margaret Gray is recorded at 33 Green Street, but not Hugh. This address could now be followed up in the census records, revealing further details which help in the search before 1855.

Turning now to street directories, a fairly easily accessible source, we can check through the annual volumes about this period to see whether any of our particular family members are listed under Gray or Dougall. Here we find in the Glasgow Directory for 1857–8:

Dougall, John, tobacconist and tallow chandler, 151/2 Main Street, Calton; house, 17 Green Street, do.

From the next year, he was in business with his brother and similar entries appear for several years and then stop. It had been known that John entered the medical profession, but this earlier involvement in business was new information. Once he had taken up medicine, he pops up again in a new guise in the Directory for 1870–1:

Dougall, John, physician and surgeon, 115 Paisley road; house, 119 do.

As you will see, he has two entries, one for his home address and the other for that of his medical practice. He was also Medical Officer of Health for Kinning Park for a number of years and since lists of such officials are included in some directories, he is also mentioned in that capacity in a section on the Burgh of Kinning Park.

Although only a small proportion of the population were eligible to vote in the nineteenth century, it may be worthwhile checking electoral registers if these are readily available. In this particular instance, John and his brother Alexander Dougall qualified to vote as joint tenants of 'works', since they rented premises for their small business. Perhaps this might have encouraged an interest in the politics of the day but who did they vote for? Something to speculate about, but certainly something to include in a narrative history of the family.

Since we know that John Dougall was a member of the medical profession, it is important to consult sources such as the 'Medical Register' and the 'Medical Directory'. Here are examples of the relevant entries in these publications, showing the difference in the amount of detail provided.

Entry from the 'medical register' for 1876

Date of Registration	Name	Residence	Qualification
1869 May 25	DOUGALL, John	115 Paisley Road, Glasgow	MB 1869, Mast. Surg. 1869, MD 1871, Univ. Glasg.

John Dougall's entry in The 'Medical Register' for 1876 was as follows:

In the 'Medical Directory' for 1875 we find a much fuller entry:

DOUGALL, John, 2, Cecil-pl. Glasgow M.D. Glasg. 1871, M.B. and C.M. 1869; (Univ. Glasg.); Sec. Glasg. Southern Med. Soc.; Mem. Gen. Counc. Univ. Glasg.; Mem. Counc. Geol. Soc. Glasg.; Mem. Nat. Hist. Soc., Chem. Sect. Philos. Soc., and Med. Chir. Soc. Glasg.; Mem. Brit. Assoc. for Adv. of Sci.; Med. Off. Health Kinning Park. Author, 'On the Relative Power of various Substances to prevent Generation of Animalculae', with special reference to the Germ Theory of Putrefaction, Trans. Brit. Assoc. Adv. Sci. 1871–2. Contrib. 'Putrefiers and Antiseptics', *Glasg. Med. Journ.* 1873; 'The Dissemination of Zymotic Diseases by Milk', Ibid, 1873; 'Case of Ovarian Dropsy during Pregnancy', *Obst. Journ. Gt. Brit.* 1874; various other Contribs. to Med. Journs.

It is clear that John was a graduate of Glasgow University and so we are led to another source the records of the university. Here is the entry from the Glasgow University Roll of Graduates. Under Dougall, John we find three entries. The first is obviously the one we are looking for, but the third, John M'Phail Dougall, was a son of the first John Dougall who also became a doctor. Here they both are:

Dougall, John, M.B., C.M. 1869, M.D. 1871. Catrine; Glasgow (Lecturer on Clinical Medicine in Royal Infirmary; Professor of Materia Medica in St Mungo's College).

Dougall, John M'Phail, M.B., C.M. 1880, M.D. 1886. Glasgow; York; Glasgow; Dunoon ; Welburn, Yorks.

As you can see, the various residences of the graduates are given.

We have now gathered a considerable amount of information about John Dougall and since he appears to be a man of some importance, it is worthwhile checking in biographical dictionaries which include figures of local significance. There is such a work for Glasgow at this period, entitled *Who's who in Glasgow in 1909*, and there we find an entry, including a photograph, and since he died in 1908 it is a very full entry covering his whole career. His year of birth is given and some details about his early life, including a mention of his father and his mother's uncle 'Sir' Duncan McArthur. Duncan was never actually knighted and some of the other information about him was inaccurate, but it was based on fact. The entry continues with mention of John's career in the soap- and candle-making business and his eventual entry into the medical profession, in which he acted as a dresser to Joseph Lister in Glasgow Royal Infirmary and received notable appointments as Medical Officer of Health for Kinning Park and Professor at the St Mungo College. A good deal of the information mentioned here had already come to light from other sources such as street directories, university records and medical directories, but to discover a biographical notice usually adds a few personal details about the individual which may be impossible to find otherwise. For example, we are told that John acted as a precentor in various churches and also that as a young man he narrowly escaped death when working in Tennant's Works at St Rollox. He rushed into a cloud of chlorine gas at a new bleaching-powder chamber and almost suffocated.

This entry was a great find and if you think a relative of yours might be included in a similar type of publication it is well worth checking. The local library or a large reference library may be able to help you here.

Individuals of this sort often receive obituaries in local newspapers and John is no exception with an obituary in the *Glasgow Herald*.

CHAPTER 7

HISTORICAL SOURCES PRE-1855

In this chapter we provide an introduction to the main sources, other than the Old Parish Registers, for the period before 1855, although some are also relevant beyond that date.

MONUMENTAL INSCRIPTIONS

As a supplement to the records of burials in the Old Parish Registers, it is well worth searching for monumental inscriptions. The information recorded on gravestones is often fuller than in a burial entry, giving the date of death rather than burial and possibly a mention of the occupation and residence of the person. Probably the biggest advantage, however, of finding an inscription from a gravestone is the likelihood that other members of the family will be mentioned. This opens up the possibilities of discovering previously unknown relatives, such as other children or parents of the deceased. Quite often the burial plot, or lair, was used by the family for several generations, so stones which pre-date the introduction of civil registration in 1855 can be particularly helpful in establishing family links which are difficult or even impossible to discover in the less reliable church registers.

To find this sort of information, you may want to wander round a peaceful country churchyard in search of your family's gravestones, but in many cases this will not be the most effective means of finding the desired details. The weather has taken its toll on many stones, which have become indecipherable, but, fortunately, a great deal of effort by various enthusiasts has resulted in the transcribing of many monumental inscriptions. Major collections of these inscriptions can be found in the Scottish Genealogy Society's library in Edinburgh, and in the National Archives of Scotland. Local libraries should also have copies of the volumes covering their own locality.

Although their significance is greater before 1855, inscriptions have continued up until the present day and so should not be ignored as a possible source for the more recent period. Since the work of transcription has concentrated on the pre-1855 stones, it may prove more difficult to trace later inscriptions. Check local libraries and archives for lists. In the cities, there are many cemeteries run by the appropriate department of the local authorities. Although they do not record the inscriptions, lists of interments have usually survived, kept either by the department or deposited in a local archives office. If you manage to track down an entry in one of these lists, it will probably give a location for the burial, where you can then look for a gravestone and maybe find a mine of information. On the other hand, on arriving at the spot, you could discover that no stone was erected. It is just one of those chances you take in the family history search.

WILLS AND TESTAMENTS

In Scotland in former times, unlike England, only moveable property such as money, furniture and equipment connected with a trade could be bequeathed in a will. As a result, land or houses could not be included and this remained the situation until after 1868. For records of the inheritance of land or houses, see the section below.

On the death of an individual, in theory someone should be appointed to administer the disposal of any moveable property and that person is named the executor. In cases where the individual left a will, an executor is usually named in it, but if there is no will, the deceased is 'intestate' and an executor is appointed by the appropriate court. Both situations require the confirmation of the executor by the court, which is how the transaction comes to be legally recorded. The resulting records are called testaments, either a testament-testamentar if there is a Will, or a testament-dative if there is none.

It is unfortunately the case that very few people left wills and even those who did may not have had an executor confirmed, but if you are lucky enough to trace some wills relating to your family you should find them good sources of genealogical and historical information.

The information usually found in testaments is the name of the deceased, date of death, confirmation of the executor, inventory of moveable property and a will if there is one. Supposing there is a will, you might find quite a number of relatives mentioned, but particularly children of the individual. This could prove some genealogical links and perhaps mention some children who do not appear in the Parish Registers. From the historical point of view, a good deal of social and economic history can be revealed, giving an idea of the social standing of your relative. You should beware, though, since because the eldest son inherited all of the land and buildings and did not receive any of the moveable property, if his father died without a Will, he may not be mentioned in the testament. Wills are the most likely source of details of your family's day-to-day life and therefore a very valuable source.

All Scottish testaments are stored in the National Archives of Scotland except for those from Orkney and Shetland, which are kept in the local archives. Before the Reformation, control over testaments was held by Church courts, but these were abolished and in 1564 Commissary Courts were established. Records survive for 22 Commissary Courts and one of their functions was to confirm testaments, with the Edinburgh Commissariot having authority throughout Scotland and for those who died abroad.

In 1823 the Sheriff Courts took over responsibility for testamentary matters.

There is a consolidated index to all Scottish testaments up to 1901 which is freely searchable on the ScotlandsPeople website. This can be searched by name, or other words included in the index, such as place or occupation. The index entries are linked to images of the wills and testaments, which can be downloaded for a standard charge. For information on confirmations after 1901, there are annual printed indexes covering the period up to 1959, which can be found in large reference libraries.

You may find it helpful to refer to *A formulary of old Scots legal documents* by Peter Gouldesborough (1985) which gives guidance on the standard format used in many Scots legal documents, including testaments and also the next two series of records to be described, Retours and sasines.

RETOURS, OR SERVICES OF HEIRS

As we mentioned in the previous section, land or houses, or 'heritable property' as it is described, could not be left in a will until after 1868. Inheritance of this type of property was recorded in the retours, or services of heirs, either special retours, which named the property, or general retours, which did not. The other details to be found are the names of the heir and the relative whose property is being inherited, their relationship and possibly the date of death of the relative.

The retours begin in 1530 and were written in Latin until 1847, except for the years 1652–9. It is important to search for a considerable period of time after the death of the earlier property owner because the retours were sometimes not recorded until well after the date of death. Although the originals are in the National Archives of Scotland, there are printed indexes which can be found in large reference libraries and these can sometimes provide sufficient detail, especially in a case when a son succeeded his father. The indexes have the added advantage of being in English. The index from 1530 to 1699 is arranged by county and gives references to two published volumes of summaries of the retours, which include most of the information. These summaries are also available in large reference libraries and a CD-ROM version has been published by the Scottish Genealogy Society. Details of which years are covered by each volume of the printed *Indexes to the services of heirs in Scotland* from 1700 onwards can be found on the National Archives of Scotland website.

SASINES

One of the most important series of records held in the National Archives of Scotland is the registers of sasines, which record the transfer of ownership of land and houses from 1617. This is a wonderful resource and there is no equivalent in England. If your family owned even a small piece of land or a small cottage, it should be possible to gather some details about them from the sasines. Quite often fathers granted land to their children and there could be a mention of previous grants with the chance of other relatives being named. Even if no family links are established in the transfer of the property concerned, there will be information about its location and boundaries (if land) and often the occupations of the two parties involved.

From 1617 to 1868 there was a General Register of Sasines, recording property in any area of Scotland and various Particular Registers of Sasines recording property in a particular county. The period 1869 onwards is covered by a register for each county. As well as these, the royal burghs had their own registers, beginning at various dates. To make a comprehensive search for the earlier period you will need to check three registers if you think your family had property in a royal burgh: firstly the Burgh Register; secondly the Particular Register of Sasines for the area concerned; and finally the General Register. If their property was outwith the royal burghs, the second and third of these will have to be consulted.

Although there are some indexes, not all areas and periods have been covered. Thhe following is a brief summary of the indexes available:

General Register	1617–1720 and 1781–1868
Particular Registers	1617–1780 some indexes, some of which have been published, and 1781–1868
Registers for each county	1869–
Burgh Registers	some indexed from 1809

The index from 1781 is arranged by country and covers both the General and Particular Registers, so this makes a search a little easier. It refers to the sasine abridgements which will probably give you all the information you require, but if you need to consult the full entries they are often in Latin. It is helpful to be familiar with the layout if you are likely to be looking at the full entries and Gouldesbrough's *Formulary of old Scots legal documents* will give you guidance here. Both persons and places are indexed for 1781–1830 and 1872 onwards, but otherwise normally just the persons are indexed. The indexes of places for large towns in some cases list specific streets, but there are also entries such as 'Glasgow: Tenements in'.

The vast majority of the sasines are kept in the National Archives of Scotland, but some Burgh Registers are in local archives, namely the register for Glasgow and the registers for Aberdeen and Dundee before 1809. The Registers of Scotland, the organisation which now deals with the registration of land ownership, is based at Erskine House in Edinburgh, but there is also an office in Glasgow which stores the sasine abridgements for the 'counties' of Dunbarton, Glasgow and Renfrew. This may prove more convenient in some cases for researchers in the west of Scotland, but the drawback is that a charge is made for each person or property searched for.

The following is an example of an entry in the sasine abridgements for Fife:

(1125) May 10. 1785.
DAVID DRYSDALE, Smith, Freuchie, and Jean Peattie, his spouse, Seised, in fee & liferent respectively, Apr. 28. 1785, – in a Tenement in FREUCHIE, par. Falkland; on Disp. by John Ramsay, Weaver, North Shields, to James Dryburgh, Merchant, Markinch, Dec. 31 1773; and Disp. & Assig. by him, Nov. 6. 1784.

P. R. 35. 205.

Sasines can sometimes be used to trace the history of a family and of land over several generations, such as in the case of the Crawfurd family of Jordanhill, where there are sasines registered in 1698, 1679, 1657 and 1628 recording the transfer of the lands of Jordanhill to various members of the family.

The sasines are in the process of being digitised and will eventually be available in digital format in the National Archives of Scotland.

REGISTERS OF DEEDS

These registers cover a wide variety of matters which involved some form of legal transaction. The most commonly recorded documents are bonds detailing loans of money while other deeds deal with settlements of testaments, marriage contracts, arrangements for apprenticeships and miscellaneous agreements between individuals. Finding a deed should fill in a little more detail of the life of the relative concerned and add some more colour to the picture you are building up.

Until 1809, deeds could be registered in any court, but from then on this function was restricted to the Court of Session, Sheriff Courts and Royal Burgh Courts. As in the case of retours, deeds are sometimes not registered until years after the transaction had taken place.

The following gives brief details of the various courts, the dates of the registers and whether they are indexed.

Registers of deeds and their indexes

Name of Court	Registers	Indexes
Court of session	From early sixteenth century	1554-95
		1705-7
		1714-15
		1750-2
		1765
		1770-present
Sheriff courts	Some from sixteenth century Some published	Very few
Royal burgh courts	Some from sixteenth century	Very few
Commissary courts	Up to 1808	Peebles, 1755-62
Local courts	Up to 1747	None

To make a thorough search, you will need to check the court of session registers and the registers for any other court covering the area in which you are interested. Most of these are in the National Archives of Scotland but there may be some in local archives. It is also worth mentioning that there are many deeds in the Gifts and Deposits Collections in the National Archives of Scotland, but it may be rather difficult to trace a relevant deed, although see the section on the Gifts and Deposits Collections on page 100.

KIRK SESSION RECORDS

These consist of the records of the body which ran the business of each Church of Scotland parish and since in the past this covered most aspects of people's lives, a great variety of information can be found there. The major items that usually appear are the organisation of relief for the poor of the parish and the disciplining of wrongdoers, with the individual's names being listed. Misconduct of parishioners might be 'breaking the Sabbath', by, perhaps, creating a disturbance when they should have been in church, or, the most commonly mentioned offence, fornication. Other matters could include lists of communicants or church members and details of the appointment of schoolmasters. These records are a major source for information on the ordinary people, containing the main listings of the poor to be found, but since they are not indexed, it can be a laborious task to search them. The National Archives of Scotland has a fairly complete collection of Kirk session records but local archives sometimes have copies.

These records have all been digitised and will be made available online, probably within the next year.

POOR RELIEF TO 1845

Up until the Poor Law Act of 1845, assistance to the poor was organised by the heritors (landowners) and the Kirk session of every parish. Sometimes separate lists were kept of payments to the poor of the parish, but more likely this information will be found mixed up with other business in the general records of the heritors and Kirk sessions. Again the main collection of these is held in the National Archives of Scotland with separate listings of heritors records and church records which include those of the Kirk sessions. In the burghs, although poor relief was dispensed, the records often give few details, but those for Edinburgh and Glasgow are rather more useful and can be found in the relevant local archive.

NONCONFORMIST RECORDS

Although in the past, the vast majority of Scots were adherents of the Church of Scotland, there were many nonconformist churches whose records have survived in varying degrees of completeness and which tend to be scattered in various locations. From the eighteenth century up until the Disruption in 1843, there were various break-aways from the established Church of Scotland with the Disruption, which resulted in the formation of the Free Church of Scotland, being the most important. After this, mergers of denominations began to take place and by 1929 many of these churches had reunited with the Church of Scotland. Many of the records of these churches are kept in the National Archives of Scotland and include baptisms, marriages and burials, lists of communicants and minute books. Two of the main churches represented are the Free Church of Scotland and the United Presbyterian Church of Scotland.

As far as the records of the Roman Catholic Church are concerned, the National Archives of Scotland have photocopies of all pre-1855 registers of baptisms, marriages and deaths, which could ease the searcher's task considerably. One register dates back to 1703, but in general they begin in the nineteenth century. The parish priests hold either the originals or copies of their own registers, while the archives of the Archdiocese of Glasgow also have registers for some of the parishes in Glasgow and the surrounding area. These have now been fully digitised, and are included on the ScotlandsPeople website.

Again, in the case of the Episcopal Church of Scotland, most of the records are still held by the local clergy, with a few originals and microfilm copies in the National Archives of Scotland. You should find the surveys of the National Register of Archives for Scotland helpful here, since all known Episcopal Church records have been surveyed and lists produced. For more information about the National Register of Archives for Scotland, see page 101.

Then there are the Baptist, Congregational, Methodist, Quaker and Unitarian churches. Some of these records are stored in the National Archives of Scotland, and Glasgow City Archives have a sizeable collection of nonconformist records for almost all churches apart from the Catholic Church. As you would expect, these cover Glasgow and surrounding areas, but the Congregational Church records come from all parts of Scotland. For the Baptist Church, the individual church should be contacted and for nonconformist records in general it is worth checking the National Register of

Archives for Scotland for possible locations, or the headquarters of the church concerned.

For records of Jews, you should consult the Scottish Jewish Archives Centre in Glasgow.

VALUATION ROLLS BEFORE 1855

Some rolls exist in the National Archives of Scotland for this earlier period, but they are isolated and sometimes they list the value of the lands but not the names of the proprietors and occupiers. The earliest of these date from 1643, while some have been published. You may find useful *A directory of land ownership in Scotland c. 1770* (Timperley 1976), which takes its information mainly from valuation rolls. The early nineteenth century is better provided for, but, as in the case of the earlier period, in the royal burghs the tax was usually paid in one lump sum and those paying were not normally listed.

If you do find family members mentioned in valuation rolls, you will probably only succeed in locating them at a particular place at a particular date since the information will be very brief and is more likely to mention proprietors than occupiers. This information might, however, provide a basis for tracing them in the registers of sasines which would give much fuller details.

For more detailed information on what is available for valuation rolls in the National Archives of Scotland, consult "Tracing your Scottish ancestors: the official guide".

HEARTH TAX AND POLL TAX

These two taxes were introduced for fairly short periods in the 1690s, the hearth tax from 1691 to 1695 and the poll tax from 1693 to 1699, and although this is a fairly serious limitation, they do provide listings of a considerable proportion of the population. All land-owners and tenants were liable to pay for the number of hearths in their houses, while the poll tax was levied on all adults who did not depend on charity. Unfortunately the records are not complete and in the case of the hearth tax, some list the amount collected but not individual's names. The arrangement of the records is by county and then by parish, with the poll tax having two series of records which both need to be checked. If you do find your family mentioned in the poll tax records, children's names may also be included.

The original documents are in the National Archives of Scotland, but there are some published lists.

TRADES

As you can imagine, those involved in trade tended to be concentrated in the royal burghs, where such matters were well regulated. In order to be allowed to practise a trade in the royal burghs, an individual was required to be admitted as a burgess. Many lists of burgesses have been published, including those for Edinburgh (1406–1841) and Glasgow (1573–1846). Otherwise, admissions can be found in burgh records, some in the National Archives of Scotland, but many in local archives. Since newly admitted burgesses were often sons or sons-in-law of burgesses, this relationship is mentioned in the records.

There also existed, in the burghs, influential craft guilds or incorporations which kept records of members, and here again they were often sons or sons-in-law of members or were apprenticed to a member of the craft. Published lists exist in some cases and the original records can be found in local archives, the National Archives of Scotland or listed in the National Register of Archives for Scotland surveys.

Because of the large proportion of burgesses and craft members who were admitted by right of their relationship to an existing member, it is possible to trace back several generations through these records, which thus can prove a very fruitful source.

John Brock was admitted as a Glasgow Burgess in 1787 as eldest son of William Brock, weaver. Checking back, we find that William had been admitted in 1776 as the eldest son of another William Brock, weaver. This William, the grandfather of John, appears in 1743 and was the eldest son of Robert Brock, deceased, gardener, who was admitted in 1719 as married to Agnes, daughter of the deceased John Duncan, gardener. We could then continue our search by following up the Duncan family. You can see the usefulness of this source, which, in this example, took us back four generations in only a few minutes of research.

The apprenticeship system was widespread until relatively recently and normally the father of the new apprentice entered into an agreement, called an indenture, with the master to whom he was apprenticed. These are mentioned in the records of the craft concerned, but not many of the indentures themselves have survived. Some appear in the register of deeds and there is a collection of Edinburgh indentures for 1613–1783 in the National Archives of Scotland. Some published lists of apprentices are available, including ones for Edinburgh (1583–1800) and Aberdeen (1622–1796). As a result of the imposition of stamp duty on indentures in 1710, there are records of Scottish apprentices for 1710–1811 in the National Archives in London. The period 1710–74 can be accessed online through the Origins Network.

Unfortunately, if your relatives were tradesmen beyond the burghs, there are unlikely to be any records available. The only sources for them are few and far between, being the records of mutual benefit societies such as the Society of Free Fishermen of Newhaven. The main repository for these is the National Archives of Scotland.

Anyone selling alcoholic drink had, from 1756, to be licensed and this covered the burghs and the counties. The granting of these licences was carried out by the burgh court or the Justices of the Peace for the county and their records are kept in the National Archives of Scotland or local archives, beginning mainly in the nineteenth century.

MERCHANT SEAMEN

Although difficult to search without fairly precise details of the ship or port concerned, there are vouchers of payments of bounties for whaling (1750–1825) and for herring fishing (1752–96). These vouchers named the crews and are available in the National Archives of Scotland.

INDEX OF BIRTHS, MARRIAGES AND DEATHS

Another source which should be mentioned is the *Scots Magazine*, which published notices of births, marriages and deaths of the more affluent sections of society. An index to these is kept in the Office of the Lord Lyon in Edinburgh for 1739–1826.

GIFTS AND DEPOSITS COLLECTIONS

This title covers a very wide range of documents which have been gifted or lent to the National Archives of Scotland by individuals, families, businesses and organisations and it may provide you with useful information, particularly if your family lived on a large estate. If the estate papers are amongst the Gifts and Deposits Collections, your family's name may well be mentioned. The online catalogue of the National Archives of Scotland allows you to search for any word or name which appears in the entry for each document in a collection. The entries include a brief description of the contents of the document and so often names may be mentioned, especially in the case of correspondence. A useful category of material found in the Gifts and Deposits Collections are wages books and these can be traced on the catalogue, although the contents are not indexed.

NATIONAL REGISTER OF ARCHIVES FOR SCOTLAND (NRAS)

You will have gathered by now that once you move beyond the three main categories of records held in New Register House, the statutory registers, census records and Old Parish Registers, most archival material is scattered in various locations. We have already looked, in Chapter 5, at how the online catalogues of the Scottish Archive Network, the National Register of Archives for Scotland and the National Register of Archives can be used to search for these. Since its foundation in 1946, the NRAS has gathered information on and conducted surveys of archive collections held outwith the National Archives of Scotland by individuals, businesses and organisations, including local authority archives. Their lists of surveys range from the very small to the very large. For example, from the one-page survey of the records of the Royal High School Athletic Club, Edinburgh, Rugby Section, to the 144-page survey of the Scottish Episcopal Church Congregations in the Diocese of Edinburgh, or large estate collections such as those of the Dukes of Hamilton, Argyll and Roxburghe.

The NRAS is administered by the National Archives of Scotland, based in its West Register House site in Charlotte Square, Edinburgh, and the index to the surveys can be consulted in the National Archives of Scotland, National Library of Scotland, many of the older university libraries and local authority archives. Any types of record can be listed and so if you have been unsuccessful in tracing a particular source in the obvious locations it is worthwhile checking the NRAS.

MAKING USE OF THE SOURCES

So we have looked at the sources, or at least the main ones, but how can you make use of what you find? The historical information giving details about the lives of your family and the environment in which they lived can be very interesting, but we would hope that you will incorporate it into some form of narrative family history.

We will describe some means of going about this in the next chapter. Before moving on to this stage, we should consider how to extend the framework of your family tree using the genealogical information you have gleaned from the sources described in Chapters 6 and 7.

The most important facts needed to make genealogical links are name, and date and place of birth or baptism, marriage and death or burial. If these are known, you will have a good chance of tracing a record of the event. This in turn may either make a genealogical link, with the parents' names given in a baptismal record or perhaps a father's name in a marriage entry, or give enough data to lead you back to an earlier event which can then establish a link. A record of burial giving the person's age may in some cases help you find the baptism, although you will probably need extra evidence to confirm this.

When tracing your family in the earlier period we have been looking at, you will very often find that only one of these important facts is known, this being the name. Everything else has to be sought out by deduction and by building up a body of evidence, similar to that in a legal case, in order to prove that each record that you find really does refer to the individual you are tracing and not to someone else of the same name.

In the case of working back from a marriage to a baptism, you will usually need to estimate the age of the bride and groom, since it is unlikely to be given. Then you can search for baptisms in the period calculated according to their estimated ages. This could range from 16 to perhaps 40, but is probably on average likely to be between 20 and 25, although average age at marriage has varied at different times in history and can also be affected by local conditions. You may have found one or both of the fathers' names in the marriage entry, which will be a big help in correctly identifying the baptism you are seeking.

The other factor, place, could also prove to be a problem. The marriage entry might state the parishes of the bride and groom, but if it does not, it is probable that the marriage took place in the bride's parish. All you can do, without evidence to the contrary, is deduce that the parish listed for each at their marriage was the one in which they were baptised. This, of course, may not be the case and when no parishes are named, the task becomes more difficult, especially in the case of the groom.

In making the connection between a baptism and the marriage of the parents, things may be a little easier. The registers can be searched for possible older brothers and sisters and then the marriage, but you may find neither these nor a marriage, since the family could have moved from another parish where the marriage and other baptisms were registered. Another possibility, if baptisms are found but no marriage, is that the parish that you are searching in was the husband's parish but the marriage took place in the wife's parish.

Although in the past movement was less common than today, especially over long distances, there was often movement in and out of parishes within a ten-mile radius, so if you lose trace of a family, you could try the few surrounding parishes.

One other consideration which may assist you is the traditional naming pattern often followed in Scotland. Further details can be found at the start of Chapter 9.

We have outlined here some of the difficulties you may encounter. You must be satisfied that you have made correct identifications for all those included in your family history. This is an area particularly studied by historical demographers in their work on nominal record linkage and its use in family reconstitution. If you want to follow up this important method of establishing reliable genealogical links, you could consult *Identifying people in the past* (Wrigley 1973), or *Nuts and bolts* (Todd 2000). Genealogists have always been used to making such links, but the historical demographers, looking at large numbers of families and making use of computers in their work, have formalised the methods. It is obviously important to make the correct links and we hope that this section has emphasised this and given you some clues on how to tackle this aspect of family history.

CHAPTER 8

PRESENTING YOUR FAMILY HISTORY

As a hunter-gatherer in the field of family history you will probably amass quite a quantity of facts. Names, dates, occupations and other snippets of information will abound, but if you have followed our advice earlier in the book, these details should be well organised and easily accessible. What will almost certainly be lacking in your collection of family history materials is narrative. You may have stories or reminiscences gathered from elderly relatives and written down or recorded digitally or on audio cassette. The collection could also include obituaries or newspaper reports about members of your family. However this sort of material is not likely to occur often and when it does, forms an isolated example of narrative. This chapter is about producing some form of continuous narrative history of your family in which you put flesh on the bones of the skeleton family tree you have constructed. In doing this, you will be able to bring together the fruits of your labours and present them in a readable form which hopefully will prove to be not only a source of satisfaction to yourself, but also of interest to relatives and perhaps even a wider audience.

WHEN SHOULD THIS BE DONE?

Obviously a reasonable amount of information is required before making a start, but to put off too long is not advisable. You may have relatives who have helped you out with facts which they can remember and documents which they own and who are keen to see the results of your investigations. It is probably unlikely that you will complete your researches for a considerable time, if ever, so do not wait for that moment, particularly considering the fact that word-processing facilities are now widely available. This makes it very easy for you to begin constructing your narrative history in the knowledge that if you discover new information, it can easily be incorporated and printed out without the need for retyping whole sections or pages. Our advice would be to compose a basic narrative as soon as possible and update it regularly. When you decide it is full enough and in a presentable form, it can be printed out and reproduced for wider circulation.

A NARRATIVE HISTORY

The simplest form of written history which you might consider using is a family tree in chart form along with associated notes on the various individuals. The names on the chart, or charts, are numbered and then on separate pages fuller details can be given for each numbered individual. These notes could range from the dates and places of birth, baptism, marriage, death and burial to extensive biographies, depending on the information you have and what you feel is appropriate.

We will now look at writing a narrative family history which may use family tree charts to increase the clarity, but with the narrative as the basis rather than in the previous format described, where the chart is the basis.

The first main type is that found in *Burke's peerage* and *Burke's landed gentry*, and in genealogy software packages. These use indentation on the page, along with various sequences of numbers and letters, to indicate different generations. The information about each individual tends to be relatively brief in this form of history.

If you are interested in using this format, have a look at some examples in Burke's publications mentioned above, which will provide a good guide as to how this method works.

James Balfour Paul wrote an introduction to Margaret Stuart's *Scottish family history* (1930), in which he describes various approaches to writing a family history. For example, the anecdotal method is usually quite easy to read, being chatty and amusing. It does not normally include many references to sources of information and does not quote from these sources to any great extent. The historical method attempts to place the family in its historical context, looking at how historical events affected the family and, perhaps, what impact the family made on history. The most comprehensive approach he calls the 'scientific method' in which all the available facts are recorded, full references to sources are provided and sources are quoted at length, possibly in a second volume containing only extracts from source materials.

You will have to make your own decision about which approach or combination of approaches you wish to take, but we would certainly hope that you would include an element of the historical method in whatever you decide upon. No family exists in a vacuum and knowledge of the community and environment in which it lives is vitally important in reaching a proper understanding of its history. By placing the family in historical context, you can pick out features which your family had in common with its surrounding community and also those features which were different. This type of approach may also help your family history appeal to local historians and others who may then be able to draw on your work to assist them with their own endeavours on a larger scale. Whatever methods you employ to write up your family history, there are a number of important points to be considered.

- You may need to decide whether to impose **censorship** on the material to be included in your history. Perhaps this will depend on who is likely to be reading the end product, but it could be that certain stories or facts gathered in the course of your researches would cause offence, so it is something worth thinking about.
- It is helpful to have clear in your mind a **procedure** for describing the history of the various branches of your family, since without a clear structure, the history could become confusing to everyone but yourself. The best plan is to begin with the earliest known ancestor, giving their story, including information about their spouse or spouses and children as they appear in the course of their life. After giving their date of death, repeat the names of their wife and children and also give brief details about any of them who will not be described more fully later. For those to be mentioned again within the text, it is useful to quote after their names the pages referring to them. In most cases it is probably best to complete one line of descent down to the most recent family members as one chapter and then consider other branches in later sections of the history.
- There are a number of **features** which you can use to improve the clarity and add to the interest of your account. Most important here are family tree charts. For a large and complicated family history you might need a main chart supplemented by others for each branch of the family. Only very brief details will be required on the charts since the individuals will be fully described in the text, but you may want to indicate the page numbers of the individuals' entries against their names on the chart.
- An **index and table of contents** are also very worthwhile if the finished work is of reasonable length. Be careful to make it very

clear in the index which particular person is being referred to, since so often there will be several family members with the same name. You could use dates, places of residence and occupations to distinguish between them.

- **References** to your sources of information should be included to either a lesser or greater extent depending on your viewpoint. To avoid interrupting the flow of your narrative, use numbers in the text, with the corresponding notes appearing at the foot of the page or at the end of either the chapter or the whole work.

- **Illustrations** will obviously increase the interest of your work and so if possible, you should include pictures of members of the family, of places where they lived, were educated and worked, churches where they were baptised and married, tombstones, medals and perhaps even coats of arms.

- Although your researches will have gathered plenty of information about the members of your family, for the purposes of a family history, particularly one using the 'historical method', you will need to build up some **background information** on the national and local history of the time. This should include not only events, but also the social and economic conditions that would affect your family. You could use a chronology such as Cheney's *A handbook of dates* to identify events of national importance. Otherwise, consult national and local histories, social and economic histories and, where appropriate, histories of occupations and institutions with which family members were associated, such as churches, schools and universities. The best place to seek advice on what sources are available is the local history or local studies section of the library for the area you are interested in. Particularly important sources for local history are the three series of statistical accounts of Scotland, with a section devoted to each parish in Scotland. The 'old' statistical account, 1791–9 and the new statistical account of 1845, have entries written by the parish ministers and vary greatly in length, depending on the interests of each minister. The third statistical account, 1951–92, was written by a variety of contributors regarded as being knowledgeable about specific areas, but is probably, at present, of less value to family historians than the two earlier 'accounts'. The relevant sections should certainly be regarded as essential reading for anyone writing a family history. The first two accounts are now available online, making them much more accessible to the general public. It is worthwhile putting some effort into this background research and should help you to produce a much better end product. This will allow you to produce a real history of your family in historical context as opposed to a mere chronicle of family events.

Two examples of narrative family histories

A reasonable strategy would be to focus on a significant ancestor. The definition of 'significant' will vary from one person's family history to another's. However, a basic definition would seem to be someone about whom you have quite a bit of detail, both in strict genealogical terms and perhaps also in terms of their work or special interests.

For example, one approach might be to look at an ancestor and write about that ancestor, his parents, siblings, spouse and children. The example given here illustrates that the narrative, as mentioned previously, is a 'work in progress' rather than a completed work. This example is written for a family readership, rather than for a wider audience.

Another possible approach could be to write up one aspect of an ancestor's life and work.

WEB PAGES

With the relatively widespread use of the Internet, a new format for presenting family history material has become available to the family historian. It has brought the possibility of personal publishing (on the Web) to a far wider public than ever before. In theory, virtually all types of material can be published on the Web: text; family trees of various sorts, both textual and graphical; other graphics, including photographs and documents; sound and video. In practice, not all of these formats are straightforward to deal with, but there is still plenty of scope for the non-specialist.

There are different ways in which you can prepare web pages. Most pages are written in HTML (Hypertext Markup Language) so you could begin by learning the basic elements of HTML and writing your own web pages from scratch. Otherwise (or in addition) you could use either a genealogy package, most of which now have the facility to create web pages, or a web editing or authoring package, the best of these at present being probably Dreamweaver, produced by Macromedia and FrontPage, produced by Microsoft. The cost implications may be important, with the financial investment in the first option being virtually zero, except perhaps to purchase one or two good books on HTML, but the investment in time learning the language being more significant. You may already be using a genealogy package for storing and organizing your

Narrative family history: An ancestor and his family

Henry Thomas Winch (1849–1899)

HENRY THOMAS WINCH was born on **11 March 1849** in Queenborough, Kent. He was **baptised on 17 April 1849** by William Worth, a Wesleyan minister.

WHO WERE HIS PARENTS?

His father was **JAMES HENRY WINCH**, a fisherman, and his mother was **ELIZABETH WINCH (née UNDERDOWN)**.

James Henry Winch and Elizabeth Underdown were married on 1 January 1844 in the parish church of Frindsbury in Kent. James Edward was the son of **EDWARD** (mariner) and **AMY WINCH**. Elizabeth Underdown was the daughter of **THOMAS UNDERDOWN** (mariner).

The witnesses to the marriage were named as Stephen and Sarah Underdown.

From the 1851 census for 127 South Street, Queenborough, Elizabeth Winch (ms Underdown) was born in Upnor, about 1820–1.

From the 1861 census, the family lived at 115 High Street.

From the 1871 census for 99 High Street, Elizabeth Winch's occupation is given as 'Linen Draper Shop Keeper'.

From the 1881 census for 99 High Street, Elizabeth Winch (ms Underdown) is, by that time, a widow and her occupation listed as 'Nurse'.

WHO WERE HIS SIBLINGS?

Henry Thomas had four sisters, **AGNES** (born in 1846–7), **ELIZABETH FANNY** (born 27 February 1852), **HARRIET LOUISA** (born 11 May 1854), **JOSEPHINE AMY** (born 13 April 1857), and a younger brother **JAMES EDWARD** (born 4 September 1860).

AGNES is only to be found so far (aged 4) in the 1851 census for 127 South Street, Queenborough – as the daughter of James Winch (fisherman – aged 39) and Elizabeth Winch (aged 30), and the elder sister of Henry Winch (aged 2). She does not appear in later censuses, and no further details are known by the family.

ELIZABETH FANNY did not marry. She was 'in service' for most of her working life. She became blind in old age and went to live with William Henry Winch (one of the sons of James Edward) and his family in 1937. Betty Cummings (ms Winch) has one or two of her personal effects, including a wooden deed box, dated 1879. Elizabeth Fanny Winch died on 5 September 1941.

HARRIET LOUISA was an 'immoveable invalid' (1881 census) and in later life was a lacemaker, living part of the year in Queenborough with one of James Edward's sons, Sid and his wife Winnie, in order to qualify for poor relief; for the rest of the year she lived in Maidstone with her brother James Edward. It is also said that she lived in a tiny cottage in Queenborough, where she did her intricate lacework by the light of a tiny oil lamp...

Narrative family history: An ancestor's life and work

The Spritsail Barge Career of Henry Thomas Winch (1849–1899)

[ADD PHOTOGRAPH HERE]

HENRY THOMAS WINCH and family lived in Queenborough, according to the 1881 census with his parents at 99 High Street, and, according to the 1891 census, at 85 High Street.

As family lore would have it, he is reputed to have had the 'freedom of the Port of London'.

Perhaps this extract from the Register of Contracts of the Watermen & Lightermen's Company throws some light on this:

	Lower Thames Street EC
Winch	Harry Keep articled Henry Thomas Winch for 2 years – commencing 9 February 1897

Normally you had to be between 14 and 20 to be bound to a Freeman of the Company and serve a five-, six- or seven year apprenticeship. Men too old to serve the apprenticeship – (Henry Thomas Winch was 47) – could serve a two-year 'contract' to a Master Waterman or Lighterman, and thereby be admitted to the 'freedom of the Company'. From the records it would appear that Henry Thomas died before completing his two-year period of being articled.

Another piece of lore was that he was master of a spritsail barge which carried china clay between Sheerness in Kent and Newhaven in Scotland. It is possible that this could have been the chalky sediment of the River Medway (known locally as the 'Mudway'), dredged to keep the channels clear and used in cement manufacture. A further possibility is that one cargo could have been shale products from the Firth of Forth area (e.g. Polkemmet), shipped from Leith. This may give a reason for being in Newhaven, Scotland in 1877, where he met his wife.

From the sole surviving family barge photograph (probably taken in the late 1880s or early 1890s), the barge pictured is a tank barge, has no davits, has capstan winches, three part vang falls, and would seem to be of about sixteen or seventeen feet beam; from its size, it would appear to have been suitable only for plying the estuarial waters of the Swale, Medway and Thames.

[ADD PHOTOGRAPH HERE]

Henry Thomas Winch, at the helm, with family,
on the River Swale, off Queenborough

At one time, the writer thought that this barge, because of its links with Queenborough, could have been the barge *Rosa* (reg. no. 78525), of thirty-six tons, built by Josiah Bird at Conyer in 1878, registered at Faversham, owned originally by F. Bunting of 34 Cyprus Road, Faversham, and which later passed into the hands of the Sheppey Glue Works at Queenborough.

According to R. H. Perks of the Society for Spritsail Barge Research:
From the Register of F. W. Monger, Inspector of nuisances at Faversham 1881–2, barges found at Faversham: *Who'd a Thout It* spritsail, built Limehouse 1825, thirty-five tons. Master Captain Winch. The barge was owned by Charles Hartnell of Limehouse, and was probably in the rubbish trade at the time of her arrival in Faversham.

East Kent Gazette – 15/1/1877. Reported the drowning of Captain James Winch of sailing barge *Alice Lloyd* of Rochester, owned by John Charles Laurence of Queenborough (who became bankrupt in June 1904). While coming back on board late at night Captain Winch jumped off the pier into his barge boat, fell overboard and was drowned. Could this be some relation? Henry Lawrence of Queenborough owned the spl *Brilliant* in 1881.

information, so it might be a good option to use this to create your web pages, but you will find that you are restricted by the predetermined format of some pages. It all depends on what you want as your end product. Software such as Dreamweaver and FrontPage is fairly costly, although there is a cut-down version of FrontPage, called FrontPage Express, included as part of Windows 98 and upwards and also of Microsoft Office 2000 Developer. The advantage of these packages is their greater sophistication and flexibility and also their ability to organize and keep control of large websites. They are recommended if you have an elaborate website in mind. Although web authoring packages are useful and increasingly powerful tools, if you wish to create more advanced web pages it is currently still beneficial to have a knowledge of HTML in order to understand the workings of the software. The software may produce a result which was not quite what you intended and a knowledge of HTML can help you to make adjustments which you may desire.

Taking all of these factors into account, our advice for the average family historian would be to use the genealogy package you have to create your web pages, but for others who require something slightly different, consider the other possibilities we have outlined.

Genealogy packages will produce family charts as web pages in many formats and for examples of these you could look at the websites describing some of these packages, listed in the software section of Cyndi's list. Drop line charts are not so commonly found on the Web although we believe that this form of graphical display of a family tree is generally the most comprehensive and easily understood means of showing family relationships. It is possible, with a bit of effort, to draw this type of family tree using a program such as the 'Draw' feature of Microsoft Word. Once the tree is completed in Word, it can then be copied and pasted into a graphics program, such as Adobe Photoshop, where it is saved as a '.gif' file, for use on a web page. It becomes more of a problem if the tree is larger than A4 size, but with some extra tinkering, a good result can be achieved. An additional feature can be added by making these 'image maps,' which allows users to click on a name on the tree which will take them to another page with text or a picture or both, relating to that individual.

As far as text, photographs, documents, sound and video are concerned, these can all be accommodated on a website and can also be produced by genealogy packages. If the results do not suit your needs and you wish to create web pages independently, you should consult the suggested reading material listed in the Bibliography.

CASE STUDY ON USING THE WEB

For a fairly straightforward example of how you could present information on web pages have a look at the *Timperley of Hintlesham* website. This has a homepage with some basic information about some of the earlier members of the family and a number of external links. One link is to another site, based in the USA, devoted to any family with the surname Timperley, others are to a site about the present day Hintlesham Hall, which is a hotel, including pictures of the house, and one to the Boughton House site. This stately home was once owned by Sir Edward Montagu, an ancestor of some of the Timperleys. You will see that some use of graphics has been made on this page. The major part of the site consists of a number of pages giving details of descendants of the family. These are displayed in the format found in Burke's peerage and now also in many reports and web pages produced by genealogy packages, using indentation to distinguish different generations. In this case they have been created in HTML format, used to display on web pages, but not from a genealogy package. This means there is greater control over how the end result looks. Very often in these types of family charts the data is displayed in one continuous sequence, using numbers and/or letters as well as indentation to help identify the various generations. This can sometimes be difficult to follow, particularly for an inexperienced reader, but the facility to link pages, which is such a basic feature of the Web, is ideal for improving the clarity of these charts. As you can see from this example, usually only three generations appear on one page. If the individuals in the second generation had many children or if there are descendants in the next generation to be shown, then a link to another page has been made to continue the line further. Using this method, it is unnecessary to use numbers or letters for different generations since such a small number of generations are displayed on one page.

The site could be developed to include more links to brief biographies of individuals, since only a few are included at present.

There is a page entitled 'Research' which describes some specific areas of research that have been done on the connected families and other pages feature two graphical family trees using drop line charts. These employ the methods we have described earlier in this chapter and the Timperley family tree is also an 'image map' with live links from names to pages with further information about the individuals. A larger example of a graphical family tree is the Crawfurd of Jordanhill family tree (see List of Websites).

There is also a picture gallery with photographs of individuals listed on the site.

Other features of the Timperley site are firstly, a page incorporating a small response form intended for those descended from the family to send in by e-mail. Secondly, there is a search page from which simple searches can be made of the site. This facility is provided free by a website search service. Finally, there is a web counter which registers the number of 'hits' on the site and gives some further information such as whether a search engine was used and what the search terms were. Again this is a free service with which you can register a non-commercial site.

As you can imagine, this site could be developed to include more external links and to use more graphics, but it should serve to illustrate a number of points of how the Web can be used for this type of information.

OTHER FORMATS

Since today it is easy to make use of various media, you might want to try your hand at using digital voice recordings, tape/slide presentations, multimedia presentations or video recordings to give your family history an added dimension. Perhaps you have already used digital voice recording or audio cassettes to record relatives' reminiscences and some local libraries keep collections of oral history recorded in one of these formats. Extracts could be used to make up an audio file or CD to accompany the text of your history, the audio equivalent of a second volume containing extracts from sources, as mentioned earlier.

Tape/slide presentations and video recordings could be used as an additional feature of a family history or, with a lot of planning, the whole work might be produced in one of these formats. Another possibility for presenting your family history to an audience is by means of 'presentation software', such as Microsoft PowerPoint, which is available both for PC and Macintosh computer systems. This software allows you to produce and show an automated slideshow, incorporating text, sound, graphics and video material. The possibilities of such a presentation are really quite impressive – you could incorporate such material as portraits or photographs of ancestors, sections of charts or trees, recordings of voices recalling events within your family history, music, video clips of people and events which have relevance to your own family history. Obviously there is scope here ranging from a fairly basic presentation to a very ambitious production depending on your talents in this field. You may well not feel the need or inclination to venture into any media other than the written word, but we mention these as possibilities which a few years ago would have been impracticable.

CHAPTER 9

FAMILY HERITAGE

WHAT'S IN A NAME?

Names, both first names and surnames, can range from the very common to the very unusual. An unusual name or combination of names can make a tremendous difference in the ability to identify the individual you are seeking. In city parishes with large numbers of baptisms, marriages and burials, there may be a number of persons of the same name registered around the same date, given that the name is a fairly common one. On the other hand, if you are searching for an unusual name, there is a much greater chance of a correct identification. Customs for choosing first names, particularly in Scotland, can also lend a helping hand to the researcher.

You may find some background information on names useful and interesting.

Originally people had only one name and surnames were adopted gradually, becoming established during the twelfth century. There are four main types of surnames: local names, relationship names, occupational names and nicknames.

The local names could refer to a place of origin, such as de Bruce, originally from Brius (now Brix) in Normandy, or a residence, such as Wood or Marsh. Nobles and great landowners who took their names from their lands were the first to have fixed surnames.

Relationship names tend to be patronymics, giving the name of the father, such as Williamson or Robertson. Since Mac means 'son of', all the names beginning with Mac are of this type, as are surnames of Irish origin, beginning with O', such as O'Brien. At one time the patronymic changed with each generation, but eventually, many became established as fixed surnames and in the case of the Scottish clans, the names beginning with Mac often refer to the individual regarded as the founder of the clan. These types of name often still changed from generation to generation in the Highlands well into the eighteenth century and in Shetland into the nineteenth century. A number of variations in patronymics can be found. Sometimes the 'son' ending was dropped, leaving the first name of the ancestor as the surname. Another variation was the shortening of the name's ending to 's': Adams, Edwards, for example.

Occupational names include Smith, Baker and Butcher, while nicknames could, among other things, refer to appearance or qualities. Amongst these type of surname are White, Long, Good and Savage. There is some doubt about how many surnames which are apparently nicknames are in fact true nicknames. It may well be that many have other derivations that are difficult to discover.

CHANGES OF NAME

Although you probably assume that your own surname has remained the same for many generations, this may not be the case since there are various reasons why surnames may change. This obviously could pose problems for the family historian, so you should be aware of the possibilities.

In the Highlands especially, when the clan system was in operation, it was common for individuals to take the surname of a powerful local clan whom they wished to support and whose protection they sought. This meant that many clansmen with names such as Campbell or Macdonald were not related to the chief they followed, but regarded themselves as part of that clan.

Another reason for changes of names was due to the fact that a sizeable proportion of the Scottish population were of Gaelic or Irish origin, often with surnames that were unfamiliar or difficult to pronounce, and these were changed to what seemed like the nearest equivalent English name. As an example, we sometimes find the Gaelic name MacDhomhnaill becoming MacDonald and the Irish name Kearney becoming Cairnie.

Corruption of names can also come about, perhaps as a result of illiteracy and local accents. An example of this is the change from some of the name Timperley to Templey, which took place during the nineteenth century.

Finally, there is the possibility that someone adopted a different surname. This might be the name of an important patron, for example Thomas Cromwell, Henry VIII's Chancellor. His nephew Richard Williams became Richard Cromwell, a direct ancestor of Oliver Cromwell. In succeeding to property, often through an heiress, the inheritor might take the name of the family whose property they were inheriting. This may actually be a condition of the inheritance. Daniel Kerr of Kersland, living in the late sixteenth century, was the eldest son of Thomas Crawfurd of Jordanhill and Janet Kerr, but took his mother's name, as she was the heiress of Robert Kerr of Kersland.

FIRST NAMES

As far as first names are concerned, you may gain some assistance from the traditional naming pattern often followed in Scotland. The eldest son was named after the father's father, the second son after the mother's father, and the third son after the father. Daughters were named after first the mother's mother, then the father's mother and thirdly the mother. This can be used as a basis to work from, but should not be relied upon and would need confirmation from another source. This could sometimes lead to duplication of names, particularly in earlier times, when the custom was more rigidly adhered to than in more recent times. Another reason for the dupli-cation of first names was the desire to ensure that a particular name survived in the next generation. As a result, if a child was in very poor health, another might be given the same name, although both might eventually develop into healthy adults.

Other sources of first names might be from friends or events, for example Victoria at the time of the Queen's coronation. Foundlings were often given the name of the place they were found or the name of a sponsor, minister or elder at the baptism. It should also be men-tioned that middle names were unusual until about 1830.

Pet names and different forms of names could prove significant in tracking down elusive relatives, some examples being Alexander/ Alastair; Agnes/Nancy; John/Ian; Jane/Jean; while Fred and Freddy could be short for either Alfred or Frederick.

THE SCOTTISH CLAN SYSTEM

Whatever its ancient origins, Celtic, Norse or Norman-French, by the thirteenth century the clan system was well established in the Highlands of Scotland. It was a distinct Gaelic tribal culture which, in its fifteenth century heyday, threatened the authority of the Stewart monarchs. Though increasingly brought into contact with the rest of Scotland, the clan system survived until its eventual dismantling, partly as a consequence of the final Jacobite uprising, which ended at Culloden in 1746.

THE CLANS – THEIR HEYDAY AND THEIR DEMISE

The clan system was part of a Gaelic tribal culture, completely separated by language, custom and geography from the Sassenach or southerner (that is, of Saxon origin – a word applicable both to the English and Lowland Scots). In Gaelic, the word *clann* means family or children. The clans lived off the land more or less self-sufficiently, with cattle as their main wealth. Stealing cattle (sometimes in order to survive) was widespread, as were territorial disputes between clans. The clansmen did not own land, only the chief, sometimes directly from the crown, sometimes from other superior clan chiefs. The most powerful chiefs in some places kept expensive courts and retainers for prestige and had virtual autonomy over matters of law and order within their territory. Not all of a clan chieftain's preoccupations were war-like. An important member of the chief's retinue was the bard, who could both compose an epic poem, perhaps recalling a feat of heroism in battle, and recite lineage, which was part of his role as the recorder of the clan's story. The clan piper was another hereditary post, of whom the MacCrimmons, hereditary pipers to the MacLeods, were the most famous. However, by the eighteenth century, with agricultural improvements spreading from the Lowlands and with some road-building taking place which made communications easier, clans and their chiefs were brought more and more into contact with 'southern' ways. Thus, even without the shock of Culloden and the violent reaction of the Lowland authorities (the banning of tartan, the forfeiting of estates, and so on), the old clan system was gradually being absorbed into a modern economic society. This process of change was noted by Sir Walter Scott in his novel *Rob Roy*, where Rob can be seen as a symbol of the old, self-sufficient ways, which contrasted with his distant cousin Bailie Nicol Jarvie, a Glasgow merchant preoccupied with progress and business. Even so, Rob also acts as a Jacobite agent and sympathiser (as did the real-life Rob Roy), demonstrating that, inevitably, the clan system was a part of Scottish politics.

THE ORIGINS OF THE CLANS

Some clans have Norman roots and married into Celtic society: Cummings (Comyns), Hays (de la Haye), Frasers (La Frezeliäre – ultimately linked to the French *la fraise*, referring to the strawberry-shaped device on the family crest), Sinclair (St Clair) and Bruce (Brix, a Normandy place name). Following early Viking raids on

Scotland, others have Norse connections: the MacLeods of Skye are said to descend from Liot, son of a Norse king; the MacDougalls of Lorne come from Dougall (Gaelic, 'dark foreigner'), grandson of Norse King Olaf, the Black. Some clans are linked with ancient monastic houses: the Macnabs, 'son of the abbot', descend from lay abbots of St Fillan on Loch Earn; the Macleans in Morven come from Gillean, who descended from the abbots of Lismore, the island in Loch Linnhe. Other examples include Macmillan, 'son of a tonsured man'; Buchanan, 'of the canon's house'; MacTaggart, 'son of a priest', and MacPherson, 'son of a parson'. Clans with uncertain origins include the MacKenzies who appeared in Ross and Cromarty, claiming descent from twelfth-century kinsman Gilleoin, as do the Mathesons, with lands close to Kyleakin in Wester Ross. The Gunns in Sutherland claim a most unusual descent: they may have been an ancient surviving Pictish tribe, forced into the far north of Scotland.

THE LORDS OF THE ISLES

Clan Donald, the Lords of the Isles, were for generations the most powerful clan in Scotland, especially on the lands by the western seaboard. Great seafarers, they controlled the sea lanes with their oared galleys (Gaelic: birlinn) about which there were many songs and tales. The power of Clan Donald was finally broken before the end of the fifteenth century, their power having brought them into conflict with the Crown.

THE MASSACRE OF GLENCOE

Clan conflict often meant spilt blood. The MacGregors are said to have massacred 140 of the Colquhouns in Glen Fruin, west of Loch Lomond. Clan Donald forces once shut one hundred Campbells in a barn near Oban and set it alight. More than one hundred Lamonts were executed at Dunoon in revenge for changing sides by the Campbells after the Battle of Inverlochy. Yet the bloody deed which has gained most notoriety was not principally a clan affair at all. The massacre of Glencoe (1692) was carried out on a branch of the Clan Donald by a regular regiment of the 'British' army, raised from the Clan Campbell. The Campbell regiment acted under orders as part of a government policy designed to bring rebel clans to heel. In this case, the brutal politics of the late seventeenth century was far more important than simply clan enmity.

THE CLANS AT CULLODEN

The powerful Clan Campbell were also to the fore at the Battle of Culloden in 1746. Their militia took the government side against the 5,000 rebel Jacobites and were part of the 9,000-strong British army which included three other regiments of Lowland Scots. Subsequent Jacobite mythology has obscured the fact that more Scots took up arms against Bonnie Prince Charlie than for him. The popular interpretation of Culloden as a Scotland–England conflict is simply a myth.

THE CLAN REVIVAL AND THE CLANS TODAY

As part of a Romantic movement in art and literature in the late eighteenth century, an interest in nature began to take root both north and south of the border. The first tourists came to Scotland, as part of a 'cult of the picturesque'. Another aspect of the Romantic movement was an interest in the idea of 'the noble savage' and thus a certain mystique became associated with the Highlands, which had been populated by a race of noble warriors. This new way of thinking, embodied in the work of Sir Walter Scott with his tales of Scottish heroes and brave deeds, received wide acclaim. In addition, by the end of the eighteenth century the Highlands were no longer seen as a threat to the nation's stability, Scotland becoming safe enough for a visit by the reigning monarch, King George IV, in 1822. The old clan ways had been swept aside by emigration, proscription following Culloden, the Industrial Revolution and 'foreign' landlords, all of which changed the nature of clans and clan lands. Queen Victoria's love of the Highlands and Balmoral and her patronage of the Braemar Highland Gathering helped sustain the fashion and the genuine interest in Scotland's Highland heritage. This has been maintained to the present day, often taking the form of clan societies, which promote the history and comradeship of the clan. Though the clans of old have gone from their homelands forever, the old traditional values of loyalty and companionship still have their place, within a family that now stretches right across the world.

IMMIGRATION AND EMIGRATION

Although both emigration from and immigration to Scotland have taken place on a fairly large scale, there are comparatively few records of this movement of population.

Via the ancestry.co.uk website, you can search incoming passenger lists for people arriving in the United Kingdom from foreign ports outside of Europe and the Mediterranean. The passenger lists cover 1878 to 1960 and may include: name of passenger; their birth date or age; port of departure; port of arrival; date of arrival; and vessel name. It is free to search the website, but there is a charge for viewing the full entry and downloading images of the passenger lists.

You can search the outward-bound passenger lists for people leaving ports in the United Kingdom and Ireland at the ancestorsonboard.com website. The lists cover 1890 to 1960 and show passengers for long-distance destinations, including Australia, Canada, India, New Zealand, South Africa and the United States of America. Again, it is free to search the site, with a charge for downloading images of the passenger lists.

If your interest lies in emigrants prior to this date, as is more than likely, there are various published lists covering emigrants to Canada and the United States, which have been compiled from various sources and are listed in the Bibliography. Having checked these, your next course of action would be to consult the immigration records of the country of destination. We recommend you check the Ellis Island website if you are interested in the period 1892–1924 since this searches, free of charge, over 22 million individuals who entered the United States of America via Ellis Island between those dates and it is also possible to search by ship names as well as by passenger name. The predecessor of Ellis Island was known as Castle Garden and there is also a freely searchable database for immigrants arriving there in the period 1830–92.

Another useful site, which provides information on emigrants to Australia, is the Public Record Office Victoria website, which has several databases covering the second half of the nineteenth century. Finally, you should also check the Ancestry website, which provides access to many passenger lists.

IRISH IMMIGRATION

During the first half of the nineteenth century in particular there was a considerable influx of Irish people into Scotland, with the main destinations being Glasgow, Edinburgh and Dundee. It can be very difficult to trace the place of origin of these immigrants since the census records usually only record the birthplace as Ireland. The most useful source is the Poor Relief applications, which record the birthplaces of many Irish people in Scotland, and this gives an added value to the database in the Glasgow City Archives, since Glasgow had the highest concentration of Irish immigrants in Scotland.

As mentioned already in Chapter 6, Glasgow City Archives have computerised indexes for Glasgow, Lanarkshire, Dunbartonshire, Renfrewshire and Bute, covering the period from the 1850s to 1900. Many Ayrshire Poor Law records have been indexed on computer for part of the nineteenth century, and are available online via the Ayrshire roots site. The records for Ardrossan in Ayrshire, in particular, are a good source for information on Irish immigrants.

Other significant groups arriving in Scotland in the eighteenth and nineteenth centuries were of Jewish and Italian origin.

JEWISH IMMIGRATION

The Scottish Jewish Archive Centre collects a wide range of material relating to all aspects of the history of the Jewish communities of Scotland and is located in Garnethill Synagogue, the oldest in Scotland, built in 1879. Its large collection is catalogued on computer, and made available to researchers.

The Historical Database of Scottish Jewry, available at the Scottish Jewish Archive Centre, collates and cross-references a wide variety of sources and lists – some 60 lists and sources, including cemetery records, synagogue registers, naturalisations, charity subscription lists and school admission registers relating to Jews in Scotland up to the 1920s. It has information on almost 16,500 individuals, and continues to grow. This database is the most comprehensive source for those who are trying to locate individuals and families during this period.

For further Jewish genealogical information and links, consult the website of the Jewish Genealogical Society of Great Britain.

ITALIAN IMMIGRATION

Italian immigration into Scotland began in the nineteenth century, but by 1890 the numbers totalled only about 750. However, by 1914 this had increased to about 4,500. Many of these 'Scots-Italians' ran small businesses as owners of cafes and ice-cream parlours and tended to form themselves into distinct communities, often intermarrying. For further Scottish Italian information and links, see the Scots Italian co.uk website.

The following two sections explain some of the historical background to the most frequent destinations for emigrants from Scotland – the Americas, Australia and New Zealand.

EMIGRATION TO THE AMERICAS

Scots were amongst the earliest settlers in North America in the early seventeenth century and it has been estimated that about 150,000 emigrated there in the period up to the American War of Independence in 1775. Some settled in colonies established by England, France and the Netherlands, but there were also efforts to set up Scots colonies in Darien (now Panama), New Jersey, Nova Scotia and South Carolina, with varying degrees of success.

Emigration took place for various reasons, but very many of the settlers were unwilling emigrants. Groups such as Covenanters, in the late-seventeenth century, and Jacobites in the eighteenth century, were banished to North America for religious and political reasons, while many other Scots left their homeland as a result of social and economic pressures, particularly due to the 'Highland Clearances' of the late-eighteenth and early-nineteenth centuries. The destinations of these emigrants were very varied, but the most popular were North and South Carolina, Georgia, New York, Nova Scotia and Jamaica.

As the nineteenth century progressed, there was a continual and significant flow of emigrants to all parts of America, continuing into the twentieth century.

EMIGRATION TO AUSTRALIA AND NEW ZEALAND

The early years of the nineteenth century, following the end of the Napoleonic Wars in 1815, saw a large increase in the British population with resultant social, economic and political problems. Emigration seemed an attractive proposition to alleviate these problems. Although originally a penal colony, Australia began to develop as a destination for free settlers and many Scots took up the offers of free land there.

The main destinations of the earliest Scottish emigrants were Tasmania, or Van Dieman's Land as it was called then, and New South Wales. During the 1820s the populations of these colonies increased by a third and in 1839, Melbourne was described as a 'Scotch Settlement'. Scots settled in various locations in mainland Australia and were numbered amongst the earliest immigrants to Queensland. Specific schemes were promoted in the 1830s to encourage unmarried women, mechanics and agricultural workers to emigrate and these, along with the social and economic conditions at home, played an important part in boosting the flow of emigrants from Scotland. A considerable proportion of these were from the Highlands, where there was little to encourage the population to stay when compared to the prospects of a new life 'down under'.

Despite the fact that government schemes aimed at encouraging emigration to Australia ended in 1841–2, a substantial flow of Scots continued to make the journey, adding to the already large Scottish contingent.

A particularly popular destination for Scots emigrants was New Zealand and by the middle of the nineteenth century about a quarter of the population was Scottish. In some years, New Zealand was the destination of more than one third of all Scottish emigrants, with Otago and the surrounding area attracting the greatest proportion until later in the century.

The contribution of Scots to the development of Australia and New Zealand was proportionally greater than that of emigrants from other parts of Britain and many of the descendants of these settlers continue to maintain a strong Scottish community sprit and pride in their Scottish origins.

HERALDRY

Heraldry, the system by which individuals and, later, organisations can be identified by a symbol known as 'arms' or 'coats of arms', developed in the twelfth century throughout Europe into a fairly standardised system. Particularly important was the fact that these arms were inherited. The original purpose was, of course, to allow noble warriors and their supporters to be identified in battle, where the arms could appear on shields, banners and tunics. Another use was on seals, authenticating important documents. Usage spread far beyond this and became a very popular means of personalising possessions, ranging from silverware and furniture to buildings.

Although only a small proportion of the population is 'armigerous', that is, has the right to use arms, you may perhaps discover at some point in your researches that you have a connection to an individual using arms. Association with a particular clan also brings up the question of the appropriate use of arms, crests and badges linked to the clan name. This section aims to give you a basic understanding of this system and how it interrelates to family history.

Firstly, it is important to be clear about some of the basic elements of heraldry. What is meant by the arms or coat of arms, the crest and the badge, and how are they used? The arms are the symbol or symbols forming a complete design, belonging to one individual, which is used on a shield, banner, tunic or elsewhere. The term 'crest' is often incorrectly used to describe the arms, but only refers to a device which sits on top of a helmet placed above a shield. Not all those bearing arms have a crest, but those who do may use it in addition to or as an alternative to their arms as a mark of personalisation. The badge, as used in Scotland, consists of a crest, surrounded by a circular strap with a buckle, which usually displays a motto. This can be worn by the supporters of the individual whose crest it features and many examples are seen in the various clan badges.

Next we will look at the various elements which can make up the arms, which can range from the simplest of designs to a complex but meaningful combination of many symbols. The 'field' is the name given to the complete area of the shield and forms the foundation of all coats of arms. On this is placed one of the tinctures. The tinctures consist of the following: five colours – azure (blue), gules (red), purpure (purple), sable (black) and vert (green); two metals – argent (silver) and or (gold); not so often found, three stains – murrey (mulberry), sanguine (blood red) and tenne (tawny orange); and the 'furs' – ermine (with variations) and vair (with variations). The reproduction of the tinctures can vary, with shades ranging from pale blue to navy in the case of azure, while argent and or are usually rendered as white and yellow. There is a general rule that one colour is not placed on another, nor a metal placed on another metal. This helps to maintain a good contrast in the design, but is not adhered to rigidly. The ermine furs have a pattern of spots and tails using black on white, white on black, black on gold or gold on black. The vair furs appear normally in white and blue, using a pattern based on squirrel skins. Each of these varieties of fur has its own name.

Once this background has been established, the next stage in creating the coat of arms involves placing 'ordinaries', 'subordinaries' and 'charges' on the shield.

The ordinaries are large, simple shapes. The following are the most commonly used:

- Pale (broad vertical band)
- Fess (broad horizontal band)
- Bend (broad diagonal band)
- Chief (broad band across top of shield)
- Cross
- Saltire (X-shaped cross)
- Pile (V-shaped triangle)

- Chevron (broad inverted V-shape)
- Pall (Y-shape)

Only one ordinary, if any, would normally be used, but a chief is often combined with another ordinary. It is also possible to have a number of these shapes in a smaller form – 'diminutives'. The shield can be divided by these shapes, for example per pale divides the shield vertically in two parts.

The subordinaries are other geometric shapes, which, unlike the ordinaries, can be used in multiples. The bordure (wide border) is one of these, others being roundels (circles) and the inescutcheon (a small shield in the centre of the main shield).

Charges could be anything else to be put on the shield. Animals and birds are commonly found charges.

Another means of varying the design is to use different types of line in dividing up a shield or outlining ordinaries and subordinaries.

Once the design of the arms is complete, it should be able to be described in a 'blazon' of the arms, that is, a standardised form of description in old French, traditionally used by heralds. First comes the field, then the ordinaries, subordinaries, charges and finally a chief or bordure, if present, and any device to be placed over the rest of the design.

It is most important to remember the principle that a coat of arms is personal to one individual. It follows from this that most arms are 'differenced'. Eldest sons inherit the arms of their fathers, but even they require differenced arms during their fathers' lifetimes. Marks of cadency provide differences between the arms of various individuals within the same family. Some of the most commonly found are: the label (a horizontal bar with three downward tabs for an eldest son, or with five tabs for a grandson), the crescent for a second son, and the molet (five-pointed star) for a third son. Once the younger sons had established their own households, they were obliged to register officially differenced coats of arms with the Court of the Lord Lyon King of Arms. These arms were often differenced by the use of variously coloured borders.

WOMEN AND ARMS

Women usually displayed arms on a lozenge rather than a shield and were entitled to use their father's arms. During their married life they could 'impale' these (place them side by side) with their husband's arms if they wished. As widows, they could also use their husband's arms. If a woman had no brothers living, or children of brothers, she had a right to use the arms of her father, either undifferenced, if she was the eldest daughter, or differenced. If the eldest daughter, she could, being an heiress, pass her arms on to her children, who could 'quarter' her arms with their father's, displaying the father's arms in the first and fourth quarters of the shield and the mother's in the second and third quarters. Sometimes individuals ended up with numerous 'quarterings' on their arms.

Responsibility for all matters heraldic in Scotland lies with the Lord Lyon King of Arms and the administration is undertaken by the Lyon Court. These matters are strictly regulated and, unlike the situation in England, all differenced versions of arms must be registered in the Lyon Court, which maintains the 'public register of all arms and bearings in Scotland' dating from 1672. This contains a considerable amount of genealogical information on the ancestry of those registering arms. Two published volumes provide details of arms from the register covering 1672–1973, while the Register for 1672 to 1907 is searchable for free on the ScotlandsPeople website. Further details and, where available, a colour illustration of the coat of arms can be downloaded for a standard charge. In addition to this, the Lyon Office records include the register of genealogies covering 1727–96 and 1823 to the present, but due to the high cost of registering genealogies, this was not used extensively. Also there are records of birth briefs, funeral entries and funeral escutcheons, again available in published form (see the Bibliography under Indexes of family histories). If you wish to pursue the study of heraldry further, you should consult the works listed in the Bibliography.

CHAPTER 10

DNA, GENETICS, HEALTH AND FAMILY MEDICAL HISTORY

DNA (deoxyribonucleic acid) plays a vital part in the makeup of every human being, because it is DNA which controls the creation and functioning of our cells. Occurring in cells throughout the body, it contains about 25 thousand genes and it is these which determine the nature of the cells and how they work. The complete set of instructions within the DNA is known as the human genome and in 2003 work was completed on creating a detailed map of it, showing where the genes are situated. Research continues into the actual function of the individual genes.

There are four different types of DNA. The first three are found in the nucleus of the body's cells and the fourth is outwith the nucleus.

- Autosomal DNA (atDNA) – contained in 22 pairs of chromosomes and controls functions such as appearance and other characteristics. Propensity to various diseases is determined by the autosomal DNA.
- Y chromosome DNA (Y-DNA) – only occurs in males and makes up one half of the twenty-third pair of chromosomes. These are the gender chromosomes, determining whether the individual is male or female. If a Y chromosome is present, the individual is male.
- X chromosome DNA (X-DNA) – makes up the other half of the twenty-third pair of chromosomes and occurs in both males and females. If there are two X chromosomes in the twenty-third pair, then the individual is female.
- Mitochondrial DNA (mtDNA) – contained in the part of the cells outwith the nucleus. Although it is found in both males and females, it can only be passed on by females.

The particular relevance of DNA to the family historian is firstly that it is inherited and secondly that it can be tested to reveal information about relationships and ancestry. Many criminal investigations now involve DNA testing to prove identity and legal cases can also make use of this to prove paternity. These tests make use of autosomal DNA and differ from DNA testing for family history, which mainly uses Y-DNA and mtDNA.

DNA TESTING FOR FAMILY HISTORIANS

The Y chromosome only occurs in males and is passed down the paternal line, normally with little or no change, from one generation to the next. As a result it is useful in identifying individuals as having the same descent in the male line.

mtDNA is only passed on by females, including to their sons, and tends to be used more for anthropological studies, which trace early ancestral origins, than for establishing relationships in more modern times.

Autosomal DNA has recently also been used for genealogical purposes, but as in the case of mtDNA, this is more useful for discovering ancestral origins. The tests provide a percentage or score indicating the likelihood of an individual's ancestry in a major population group or a region of the world. The results may indicate origins in more than one of these, for example 80 per cent East Asian, 20 per cent Indo-European. Unfortunately it is not possible to tell whether the ancestry is from recent times or ancient times.

Testing kits normally consist of a swab which is rubbed around the inside of the cheek and then placed inside a tube containing a liquid which preserves the sample until it reaches the laboratory. This means it is a very easy process to provide a sample and does not involve taking blood.

Y-DNA TESTING

Since this type of testing is currently the most useful for the purposes of family historians, we will look in a little more detail at the processes involved.

When the analysis of the sample is carried out, recordings are made at a number of markers located at different points along the chromosome. The number of markers tested vary from one organisation to another and often an organisation will offer tests on different numbers of markers, with payment graded accordingly. For example, it is possible to have 12, 27, 37 or 67 marker tests. The more markers tested, the more precise the information obtained.

Since the Y chromosome is passed down through the male line, with normally very little change over a number of generations, this helps to establish descents from a common ancestor in the male line. There are, however, two types of mutation which can occur in the Y chromosome – SNPs (single nucleotide polymorphisms) or 'Snips', which are very rare and might happen every thousand years or more, and changes in STRs (short tandem repeats), which happen more frequently. SNPs affect fairly large groups of people and allow geneticists to categorise populations into haplogroups, for example the R1b haplogroup, which is the most common haplogroup in Western Europe.

Four chemicals appear at each marker – adenine, thymine, cytosine and guanine – and these are given the codes A, T, C and G. The pattern of the code is recorded at specified markers and within this pattern are found repeats, such as GATAGATAGATAGATAGATAGATA, which would be recorded as having the value 6 at the marker being tested. The significant information reported in results from the tests on each marker is the number of times the same pattern of code is repeated. This is known as the haplotype. The results quote the marker and then the marker value, for example DYS 393 13, DYS 390 25 and so on. The DYS stands for DNA Y chromosome segment, so at marker 393 there are 13 repeats. If there is an exact match at all the markers between two or more samples of DNA, then the individuals are descended from a common ancestor in the male line, probably in fairly recent times. Supposing there are some minor differences, the individuals may still share a male line descent from a common ancestor, but the fact that there have been some changes in the STRs shows that the most recent common ancestor (MRCA) is more remote in time. Because the changes occur at random, it is difficult to accurately estimate the time from the most recent common ancestor (TMRCA), but the more markers that are tested, the more accurate these estimates can be. With tests currently available, it should be possible to be fairly confident that two individuals with closely matching results have a MRCA at about 250 to 300 years ago.

There are now several organisations studying genetics purely for the purposes of family history. Family Tree DNA is a commercial company based in the USA and claims to have the largest DNA database in the field of genetic genealogy, with over 260,000 records. It offers Y-DNA tests on 12, 37 and 67 markers, mtDNA tests and autosomal tests.

In the UK, Oxford Ancestors, the company founded by Bryan Sykes, Professor of Human Genetics at Oxford University and author of *The seven daughters of Eve* and *Blood of the Isles*, offers similar services specifically for genealogists, while EthnoAncestry in Edinburgh offers 27 marker tests.

The Sorenson Molecular Genealogy Foundation is a non-profit-making organisation based in Salt Lake City which collects DNA samples and associated genealogical information. So far, it has gathered over 90,000 DNA samples along with four generation pedigrees contributed by volunteers worldwide. Two databases of results are searchable online, the Y-chromosome database and mitochondrial database. It is also performing research on autosomal DNA which so far only extends back to the grandparent generation.

Another interesting project is the Genographic Project, which is being run by National Geographic and IBM. The aim is to map the origins and migrations of early man and involves the collection of DNA samples from indigenous populations throughout the world and the analysis of DNA from ancient remains. The general public also has the opportunity to buy a testing kit and send in a sample: see the Family Tree DNA website.

GENETIC GENEALOGY PROJECTS

Many individual surnames now have their own DNA projects and a list of many of these is available on the Family Tree DNA website. It is worth mentioning here a few projects of particular Scottish interest.

The Scottish Clans DNA Project was set up in 2001, originally to try to establish relationships between those bearing clan names, using DNA test results, but has been widened to include those of Scottish, Irish, British and Scandinavian origin. It is still relatively small scale, with about 2500 results included on the database.

Also set up in 2001, the Clan Donald DNA Project now boasts over 700 participants and is the largest family-based genetic genealogy project. In 2004 the project produced a DNA profile for Somerled, Lord of the Isles (d. 1164), regarded as the ancestor of the MacDonalds, MacDougalls and MacAllisters. Work is continuing, to establish links between the various branches of these clans.

Although based in Ireland, research undertaken by the Niall of the Nine Hostages DNA Project at Trinity College, Dublin, has a good deal of relevance for Scots. It has discovered that a considerable number of Irish men, possibly one in twelve, have the same Y chromosome, as well as a good number in Scotland. It is thought that they may all descend in the male line from Niall of the Nine

Hostages, the famous fifth century Irish tribal leader. His descendants were the dominant rulers in Ireland until the eleventh century. You can check the 12 marker or 25 marker tests on the Family Tree DNA website, to see if your own DNA matches up.

CASE HISTORIES

There are a number of notable case histories involving the use of DNA testing of which the following are interesting examples.

The case of the Romanov family, Tsar Nicholas II of Russia, his wife and children, who were shot by the Bolsheviks in the Russian Revolution in 1918, is well known. Claims were made that one or more of the family had survived the firing squad, in particular a woman named Anna Anderson, living in America, who claimed to be Princess Anastasia. With the newly developed techniques of DNA testing, research was carried out a few years ago, including the testing of Prince Philip, Duke of Edinburgh's DNA, since he was closely related to the Romanovs. This finally established that Anna Anderson was not Princess Anastasia.

The remains of Cheddar Man were found in a stone age burial site in Somerset dating from around 7000 BC. By extracting DNA from the remains and comparing it with samples from residents of the locality, it was discovered that a school teacher named Adrian Targett was actually related to Cheddar Man.

Also in Somerset were found the remains of Bleadon Man, who died over 2000 years ago. Once again, DNA tests have revealed that there are several people still living in Bleadon who are related to Bleadon Man.

GENETICS AND HEALTH

A number of projects are now in progress, looking at the genetic aspects of health, and it is useful to be aware of these, although they are not specifically concerned with genealogy. Their particular focus is in researching the genetic factors relating to diseases and how this knowledge can be applied to the development of appropriate treatments for these.

One of the longest-running projects is deCODE Genetics. This is a commercial company based in Iceland which aims to develop drugs based on genetic research into common diseases, such as heart attack, stroke, Alzheimer's disease, osteoporosis and asthma. Due to the fact that Iceland has seen little immigration over the last 1100 years and has good genealogical data and health data, it provides a good environment for this type of research. The company uses this information in conjunction with data gathered from volunteers, to help pinpoint specific genes which predispose families to particular diseases. So far they have gathered data from over 100,000 volunteers, which is more than 50 per cent of the adult population, and is currently developing drugs aimed at combating heart attack, arterial thrombosis and other diseases.

The Estonian Genome Project was set up by the Estonian government in 2001 and is now run by a research institution within the University of Tartu. It has very similar aims to those of deCODE Genetics and at present has collected about 20,000 samples. The hope is that around 100,000 samples will be gathered by 2011–12.

In the UK there is now a much larger project, called UK Biobank. This aims to use 500,000 volunteers aged 40 to 69 to study the effects of lifestyle, environment and genes on health. The participants' health will be studied over a period of many years. At present, almost 200,000 volunteers have been recruited.

A complementary study named Generation Scotland was launched in 2006, and focuses particularly on the genetic causes of specific diseases, rather than considering the effects of lifestyle and environment, as does UK Biobank.

MEDICAL FAMILY HISTORY

It has been known for long enough that some diseases and medical conditions can be inherited and, probably encouraged by the tremendous advances over the last few years in tracking down the genetic origins of various diseases, there has been an increasing interest in the tracing and recording of family medical history. The value of this is becoming more evident as the prospect of new treatments and even cures becomes a real possibility. Perhaps by researching the diseases of past members of your family, you may be able to discover the likely health problems of present and future generations, making it much easier to identify any appropriate new treatments which could even in some cases save lives. There is even a book on this topic subtitled *How tracing your family medical history can save your life* (Daus 1999).

There is a particular form of family tree chart that has been developed for the purposes of medical genealogy, where the aim is to record information relating to the medical history of a family. Genograms usually display four generations, partly due to the fact that details of medical history are rarely available before this point and particular symbols are used to indicate various medical diseases or conditions.

The standard symbols used in a genogram are:

- a circle for a female
- a square for a male
- a cross through one of the above, indicating the person is dead
- a horizontal solid line connecting two people, indicating a marriage
- a horizontal solid line which is slashed, indicating a divorce or non-committed relationship
- a vertical or diagonal solid line, indicating a biological connection
- a vertical or diagonal dashed line, indicating a special relationship such as adoption

If you are interested in this aspect of family history, specially designed software is available for recording family health history and creating genograms, such as GenoPro.

The realisation that technology in this field is developing quickly may lead to the development of gene banking. This involves the storing of DNA samples in the hope that at some point in the future, newly developed tests can be applied to these samples, which might pinpoint genetic causes of diseases and medical conditions. This could allow relatives of the donors of the DNA samples and others with the same genes to benefit from new treatments.

The advances in genetics have been enormous over the last fifty years, so who can tell what further developments may be made and whether some of these might assist family historians? All we can say is: watch this space.

ENGLISH, WELSH AND IRISH RECORDS

ENGLISH AND WELSH RECORDS

The civil registers in England do begin earlier (1837) than those in Scotland, but provide less information. The birth certificates do not give the date and place of the parents' marriage, the marriage certificates only give the names of the fathers of the bride and groom, and the death certificates do not give any parents' names at all.

The procedure for searching the civil registers is also rather different. Indexes are available at the National Archives at Kew and on microfiche at various major libraries, but the easiest means of searching for a birth, marriage or death in England and Wales from 1837 is online. The freely available FreeBMD index to the civil registers is almost complete up to 1930 while various commercial organisations provide searches on the indexes almost up to the present day. These include Ancestry, BMDindex and Findmypast.com.

If you find an entry in which you are interested, you must then apply for an official copy of the certificate, which can be done online at the General Register Office website. Searching in this way can take very much longer than a day's search in the ScotlandsPeople Centre, where you can verify entries as you go.

There is a desire to produce an official online index with linked images, an equivalent to ScotlandsPeople, but plans are uncertain and the completion of any such project would not be achieved in the short term.

CENSUS RECORDS

There is little to say about the content of the census records since these are virtually the same as those for Scotland and are kept in the National Archives. As already described in Chapter 3, the 1881 British census on CD-ROM covers England and Wales as well as

Scotland. The English and Welsh portion is available online on the FamilySearch website.

All of the census records from 1841 to 1911 are available online via The National Archives website, with free index searches and payment required for further details. These include the opportunity to download images from the schedules. The free index searches return varying amounts of information for different years, with 1881, 1901 and 1911 being the most generous.

INTERNATIONAL GENEALOGICAL INDEX

The IGI is available on the Internet, but the coverage is rather patchy compared to that in Scotland.

EARLIER RECORDS

When we come to the earlier records, we see a contrast between the centralisation of many of the Scottish sources in the General Register Office for Scotland and the National Archives of Scotland and the decentralisation in England and Wales, with much being kept in the local archives or record offices. In particular the parish registers are held in the local offices. Many more of these have earlier starting dates than in Scotland, with 1538 or 1558 being fairly common.

WILLS AND ADMINISTRATIONS

Other major sources are wills and administrations, marriage licences and land records. Wills and administrations (granted for those not leaving a will) are stored centrally at the Probate Department of the Principal Probate Registry Family Division, London, from 1858, but before that may be found in several locations. For more information on how to locate these you could consult *Wills and probate records: a guide for family historians* (Taylor and Grannum 2009). The National Archives have made the Prerogative Court of Canterbury wills available online covering the period 1384–1858. There is a free index search and the linked images of the wills can be downloaded for a standard charge.

MARRIAGE LICENCES

In Scotland, marriages were authorised by the proclamation of banns, but in England there was the alternative of having a marriage licence granted. These are found mainly in local archives or record offices and some have been published. Often they give the occupation of the groom and names the place or places where the marriage might take place. In a situation where one or both of the couple were under age, the consent of the parents would be required and so in most cases the father's name would be given. An online database of the Vicar-General and Faculty Office marriage licences for 1694–1850 is available through the Origins Network. This covers mainly well-off families and those living in the London area.

LAND RECORDS

These are nothing like as complete as in Scotland. The main sources are the manorial court rolls, which have survived for some areas, but are haphazard compared to the sasines.

ONLINE SOURCES

Many other online databases can assist in English and Welsh family history research, in particular Boyd's Marriage Index, an important source for many parts of England, and the National Burial Index on findmypast.com, which complements the IGI, since it does not include deaths and burials in significant numbers. In addition to these, a large collection of data from parish registers on findmypast. com and non-conformist church registers on BMDregisters.co.uk can be accessed, but of course payment is required.

IRISH RECORDS

To begin with, the bad news. Unfortunately many Irish records were lost in 1922 when the Four Courts in Dublin were destroyed. Amongst these were almost all Irish wills and about 1,000 Protestant church registers of baptisms, marriages and burials. Now let's look at what does survive.

Civil registration began in 1864, giving the same information as English civil registration, but marriages celebrated in Protestant churches had been registered since 1845.

All these records are in the General Register Office of Ireland in Dublin, except for the civil registers covering Northern Ireland from 1922, which are only held in the General Register Office (Northern Ireland) in Belfast. The Northern Ireland Office also holds copies of all the earlier civil registers for that area. Indexes to the records of civil registration 1845–1958 are freely available online on the Family Search pilotsite.

The Ulster Historical Foundation provides a database of births and marriages taken from the civil registers and some church registers for County Antrim, County Down and Belfast up to 1921 and of burials mainly for Belfast. Payment is required beyond the free index search.

CENSUS RECORDS

The census records for 1901 and 1911 have survived, but before this, little exists. The various websites on Irish family history give details of earlier census fragments and 'census substitutes'. All census records are held in the National Archives in Dublin, who are making the full details of the 1911 census and 1901 census available online completely free. At the time of writing, the 1911 census is accessible.

Because of the lack of these records, two sets of land records have assumed greater importance, the Tithe Applotment books and Griffith's Valuation. The Tithe Applotment books, covering the period 1824–37 (available online via Ancestry), give the names of the occupiers of lands, the area of land and the tithes payable to the Church of Ireland. These are not comprehensive, however. Griffith's Valuation, published between 1847 and 1864, gives a valuation of all property in Ireland, listing the names and addresses of all landlords and tenants. A free version of this is available on the Internet.

CHURCH REGISTERS

The coverage of church registers is not good, with only a few Roman Catholic registers before 1820. There are microfilm copies of these in the National Library of Ireland, Dublin. For the Church of Ireland, the Irish branch of the Anglican Church, about 600 registers have survived for about a third of the parishes and are held by the local churches, or in the National Archives of Ireland, Dublin. The National Archives maintains lists of all the registers that have survived. Many of the Presbyterian church records are held by either the local churches or the Presbyterian Historical Society in Belfast. The Ulster Historical Foundation databases include baptism and marriage records from some church registers.

ULSTER COVENANT AND FREEHOLDER RECORDS

The first of these two useful online sources contains the signatures and addresses of just under half a million opponents of the Irish home rule measures of 1912. Although confined mainly to the Protestant section of the community, this does cover a substantial percentage of the population.

The Freeholders records database is an index to pre-1840 registers of those registered to vote and Poll books of those who actually voted.

WILLS

Although very many of these were destroyed, the situation is not quite as bad as it might seem at first. There is still an index, published in 1897, entitled 'Index to Prerogative Wills of Ireland, 1536–1810' by Vicars and also the Betham extracts of wills – extracts of genealogical information from almost all wills proved in the Prerogative Court of Armagh, 1536–1800. These are mainly confined to wills of those with property in more than one diocese. There are copies of these extracts in the National Archives, Dublin, with associated pedigrees held in the Genealogical Office, within the National Library of Ireland, also in Dublin.

The indexes of wills and administrations proved in the consistory courts and the prerogative court up to 1857 have survived and are in the National Archives. There is now an online index to copies and extracts of pre-1858 wills held by the Public Record Office of Northern Ireland.

From 1858 onwards there are indexes of wills and administrations in the National Archives in Dublin and the Public Record Office of Northern Ireland, giving the date and place of death and occupation of the individual along with the names and addresses of the executors. Some copies of wills for this period are also available at these two repositories. As the first stage of an ongoing project, online indexes to the wills proved in the District Probate Registries of Armagh, Belfast and Londonderry from 1858 to c. 1900 are available online. At a later stage, these index entries will be linked to images of the wills themselves.

MARRIAGE LICENCES

The prerogative marriage licences for 1630–1858 and the Ossory consistory licences for 1734–1808 are kept in the Genealogical Office.

Indexes for about a dozen dioceses, covering the period up to 1857, are available in the National Archives, while some have been printed up to 1800.

MONUMENTAL INSCRIPTIONS

As in Scotland, many inscriptions have been recorded and published and can prove a useful source. The History from Headstones website has an online database indexing many of these.

INTERPRETING OLDER FORMS OF HANDWRITING

As your researches take you back in time, the problem of reading the handwriting becomes more acute, because, although even relatively recent documents may sometimes be difficult to read, in earlier documents you have different forms of letters and even sometimes different languages to contend with.

The most common style of handwriting used in official documents from about 1600 to about 1750 was 'secretary hand'. Some of the common letter forms are different from those of today, in particular the letters e, h, r and s.

It has been stated by Johnson and Jenkinson in their *English court hand* (1915) that 'it is not too much to say that you cannot read a word with certainty unless you know what it is'. To achieve this, try to familiarise yourself with the type of document you will be reading, for example, parish register, Kirk session records, a testament, a sasine. It may well follow a standard format, including abbreviations. You may find it helpful to refer to a Scots and perhaps a Latin dictionary, legal word lists and glossaries. It is even more important to build up this background knowledge if you are tackling documents in Latin.

Despite what we have just said, do not be put off by feeling there is a tremendous amount of study to be undertaken before even starting to read a document. If you are unable to spend this time, it is still often possible to achieve a lot through sheer perseverance.

PROBLEM WORDS

These may occur for several reasons:

- **Interference** may be caused by descending letters from above or ascending letters from below. Be careful not to regard these as part of the word you are trying to decipher.

- **Abbreviations** – Widespread use was made of these in earlier times. There may be telltale marks indicating that an abbreviation has been used. A 'mark of suspension' shows where letters are missing from the end of a word. The mark is usually a flourish from the last written letter. A 'mark of contraction' shows where letters are missing from the middle of a word. This mark is usually above the line. Common omissions are the letters m and n. Words beginning with p may be abbreviations for the prefixes pro, pre or per. A superscript letter could also indicate an abbreviation, especially after the now obsolete letter 'thorn', for example Yt = that.
- **Different spellings**. Remember that spelling in the past was not standardised as it is today, so be prepared for variant spellings.
- **Non-English words**. There could be Scots words or Latin words and for these you might want to consult Scots or Latin dictionaries.
- **Legal terms**. You could consult the SCAN glossary or books mentioned in the Bibliography.
- **Numerals**. These are usually written as Roman numerals and if there is an i at the end of the numeral, it appears as a j.
- **Dates**. Sometimes you may find a year written in a strange mixture of Roman numerals and words. This includes the use of three elements, firstly jaj meaning 1000, secondly the Roman numeral v, vi or vij (5, 6 or 7) and C (for 100) with a mark of contraction, then the rest in words, For example jajvijC + twentie (1720).

It is a good idea to compare individual words and letters to see whether they are more legible elsewhere in the document. The context in which a word appears can also help in working out a difficult word. Try putting the document aside for a time and return to it later, when a second reading may fill in gaps from the first reading. With practice you will find that you become more accustomed to reading old documents.

For further help in the study of handwriting, or palaeography, you could consult the selection of books listed in the Bibliography, the Scottish Handwriting website and the National Archives web pages on 'Palaeography: Reading old handwriting 1500–1800'. Courses are also available on the subject.

WEBSITES

ARCHIVES

Aberdeen City Archives
http://www.aberdeencity.gov.uk/LocalHistory/RM/loc_ArchivesHomePage.asp

Access to Archives (A2A)
http://www.nationalarchives.gov.uk/a2a/

Advocates Library
http://www.advocates.org.uk/library/index.html

Angus Archives
http://www.angus.gov.uk/history/archives

Archives Hub
http://www.archiveshub.ac.uk

Argyll and Bute Council Archives
http://www.argyll-bute.gov.uk/content/atoz/services/archives

Ayrshire Archives Centre
http://www.ayrshirearchives.org.uk

Bank of Scotland
see Halifax and Bank of Scotland

Clackmannanshire Archives
http://www.clacksweb.org.uk/culture/archives

Dumfries and Galloway Archives
http://www.dumgal.gov.uk/index.aspx?articleid=2300

Dundee City Archive and Record Centre
http://www.dundeecity.gov.uk/archive

East Dunbartonshire Archives
http://www.eastdunbarton.gov.uk/archives

Edinburgh City Archives
http://www.edinburgh.gov.uk/internet/a-z/AZ_archive

Falkirk Council Archive
http://www.falkirk.gov.uk/services/community/cultural_
services/museums/archives/archive.aspx

Fife Council Archive Centre
http://www.fife.gov.uk

General Register Office, Dublin
http://www.groireland.ie

General Register Office for England and Wales
http://www.gro.gov.uk/gro/content/births/obtainingbirth
certificates/index.asp

General Register Office for Scotland
http://www.gro-scotland.gov.uk

General Register Office (Northern Ireland)
http://www.groni.gov.uk

Glasgow Archdiocese (Roman Catholic), Archdiocesan Archive
http://www.rcag.org.uk/history_intro.htm

Glasgow City Archives
http://www.glasgow.gov.uk/en/Residents/Library_Services/
The_Mitchell/Archives

Halifax and Bank of Scotland Group Archives
http://www.lloydsbankinggroup.com/about_us/company_
heritage/Group_Archives/halifax_bos_group_archives.asp

Highland Council Archive Service
http://www.highland.gov.uk/leisureandtourism/what-to-see/
archives

Lochaber Archive Service
http://www.highland.gov.uk/leisureandtourism/what-to-see/
archives/lochaberarchives

Lothian Health Services Archive
http://www.lhsa.lib.ed.ac.uk

Maritime history archive: Memorial University of Newfoundland
http://www.mun.ca/mha/index.php

Moray Council Local Heritage Centre
http://www.moray.gov.uk/LocalHeritage

National Archives, London
http://www.nationalarchives.gov.uk

National Archives of Ireland, Dublin
http://www.nationalarchives.ie

National Archives of Scotland
http://www.nas.gov.uk

National Library of Ireland
http://www.nli.ie

National Library of Scotland
http://www.nls.uk

National Maritime Museum, London
http://www.nmm.ac.uk

National Register of Archives
http://www.nra.nationalarchives.gov.uk/nra

National Register of Archives for Scotland
http://www.nas.gov.uk/onlineRegister

NHS Greater Glasgow and Clyde Board Archive
http://www.archives.gla.ac.uk/gghb

North Highland Archive
http://www.highland.gov.uk/leisureandtourism/what-to-see/
archives/northhighlandarchives

North Lanarkshire Archives
http://www.northlan.gov.uk

Orkney Archive
http://www.orkneylibrary.org.uk/html/archive.htm

Perth and Kinross Council Archive
http://www.pkc.gov.uk/library/archive.htm

Presbyterian Historical Society, Belfast
http://www.presbyterianhistoryireland.com/index.php?id=3

Principal Registry of the Family Division
http://www.courtservice.gov.uk/cms/wills.htm

Property Registration Authority, Dublin
http://www.landregistry.ie

Public Record Office of Northern Ireland
  http://www.proni.gov.uk

Registers of Scotland
  http://www.ros.gov.uk

Registrar of Births, Deaths and Marriages, Dundee
  http://www.dundeecity.gov.uk/registrars

Royal Bank of Scotland Group Archives
  http://www.rbs.com/about-rbs/g1/heritage.ashx

Royal College of Physicians and Surgeons of Glasgow
  http://www.rcpsg.ac.uk/FellowsandMembers/ArchiveServices/
    Pages/mem_sparchiveintroduction.aspx

Royal College of Physicians of Edinburgh
  http://www.rcpe.ac.uk/library/index.php

Royal College of Surgeons of Edinburgh
  http://www.rcsed.ac.uk/site/297/default.aspx

ScotlandsPeople Centre
  http://www.scotlandspeoplehub.gov.uk

Scottish Archive Network
  http://www.scan.org.uk

Scottish Borders Archive and Local History Centre
  http://www.scotborders.gov.uk/council/specialinterest/heart
    ofhawick/index.html

Scottish Jewish Archives Centre
  http://www.sjac.org.uk

Shetland Archives
  http://www.shetland.gov.uk/archives

Signet Library
  http://www.signetlibrary.co.uk/index.asp?cat=Library

Stirling Council Archives Services
  http://www.stirling.gov.uk/index/stirling/archives.htm

Strathclyde Area Genealogy Centre
  http://www.glasgow.gov.uk/en/Residents/
    BirthDeathMarriage_Citizenship/GenealogyCentre

University of Glasgow Archive Services
  http://www.gla.ac.uk/archives

West Lothian Council, Archives and Records Centre
  http://www.wlonline.org.uk/tourism/FamHistGenInfo

BACKGROUND

Histpop – the online historical population reports website
  http://www.histpop.org

MeasuringWorth
  http://www.measuringworth.com

National Archives: currency converter
  http://www.nationalarchives.gov.uk/currency

Statistical accounts of Scotland 1791–9 and 1845
  http://edina.ac.uk/StatAcc

Vision of Britain through time
  http://www.visionofbritain.org.uk

BIBLIOGRAPHIES

Bibliography of Scotland – part of Scottish Bibliographies Online
  http://sbo.nls.uk/cgi-bin/Pwebrecon.cgi?DB=local&PAGE=First

Periodical Source Index (PERSI)
  Available online via Ancestry, http://www.ancestry.co.uk

Royal Historical Society bibliography
  http://www.rhs.ac.uk/bibl/bibwel.asp

BIOGRAPHIES

Oxford dictionary of national biography
  http://www.oxforddnb.com/public/index.html?url=%2Findex.jsp

Who's who in Glasgow in 1909
  http://gdl.cdlr.strath.ac.uk/eyrwho

COMPUTERS

BBC Internet introduction
  http://www.bbc.co.uk/webwise

Family Tree Maker
http://www.familytreemaker.com

MyFamily.com Internet community for families
http://www.myfamily.com

Personal Ancestral File (PAF) free download
http://www.familysearch.org

Reunion
http://www.leisterpro.com

TONIC basic course on Internet use
http://www.netskills.ac.uk/onlinecourses/tonic

EMIGRATION AND IMMIGRATION

Ancestorsonboard: UK outbound passenger lists 1890–1960
http://www.ancestorsonboard.com

Castle Garden
http://www.castlegarden.org

Convict transportation registers database
http://www.slq.qld.gov.au/info/fh/convicts

Dobson, David
http://www.btinternet.com/~lds.dobson

Ellis Island
http://www.ellisisland.org

Index to unassisted inward passenger lists to Victoria (Australia) 1852–1923
http://proarchives.imagineering.com.au

Jewish Genealogical Society of Great Britain
http://www.jgsgb.org.uk

Scotsitalian.co.uk
http://members.lycos.co.uk/scots_italian

UK inbound passenger lists, 1878–1960
Available online via Ancestry, http://www.ancestry.co.uk

FAMILY HISTORY GUIDES

FamilySearch research helps
http://www.familysearch.org

GENUKI
http://www.genuki.org.uk

GENERAL GENEALOGY SITES

Cyndi's List of genealogy sites on the Internet
http://www.cyndislist.com

RootsWeb
http://www.rootsweb.ancestry.com

Scottish Family History: University of Strathclyde Library
http://www.strath.ac.uk/jhlibrary/sr/scotfam

GENETICS

DeCODE Genetics
http://www.decode.com

Estonian Genome Foundation
http://www.genomics.ee/index.php?lang=eng&PHPSESSID=fcaa
d34e95aac7f6054240712fd2606e

EthnoAncestry
http://www.scotsfamily.com/dna-testing.htm

Family Tree DNA
http://www.familytreedna.com

Generation Scotland
http://www.generationscotland.org

Genographic Project
http://www.familytreedna.com/ftdna_genographic.html

Genopro
http://www.genopro.com

Oxford Ancestors
http://www.oxfordancestors.com

Sorenson Molecular Genealogy Foundation
http://www.smgf.org

UK Biobank
http://www.ukbiobank.ac.uk

HANDWRITING

National Archives: Palaeography tutorial
http://www.nationalarchives.gov.uk/palaeography

Scottish Handwriting.com
http://www.scottishhandwriting.com

HISTORICAL DEMOGRAPHY

Cambridge Group for the History of Population and Social Structure
http://www.hpss.geog.cam.ac.uk

LIBRARY CATALOGUES

British Library
http://blpc.bl.uk

CAIRNS
http://cairns.lib.strath.ac.uk

Copac
http://www.copac.ac.uk

Library of Congress (USA) Online Catalog
http://catalog.loc.gov

National Library of Scotland
http://www.nls.uk

WorldCat
http://www.worldcat.org

MAILING LISTS AND FORUMS

Cyndi's List mailing lists
http://www.cyndislist.com/mailing.htm

GENBRIT mailing list for British genealogy
http://lists.rootsweb.ancestry.com/index/intl/UK/GENBRIT.html

GenForum
http://genforum.genealogy.com

RootsWeb mailing lists
http://lists.rootsweb.ancestry.com

ORIGINAL SOURCES

1851 Co. Antrim Census remains of the Census
http://irishgenealogy.net/cp/phpbb3/viewforum.php?f=34

Addison, W. Innes (compiler) (1898) **A roll of the graduates of the University of Glasgow from 1727 to 1897**
http://www.archive.org/details/rollofgraduatesooounivrich

Addison, W. Innes (ed.) (1913) **The matriculation albums of the University of Glasgow from 1728 to 1858**
http://www.archive.org/details/matriculationalboounivuoft

Ancestorsonboard: UK outbound passenger lists 1890–1960
http://www.ancestorsonboard.com

Ancestry.co.uk
http://www.ancestry.co.uk

Ancestry.com
http://www.ancestry.com

Anderson, James R. (ed.) (1923–5) **The burgesses & guild brethren of Glasgow, 1573–1750**
http://www.archive.org/details/scottishrecordso43scotuoft

Anderson, Peter John and Johnstone, James Fowler Kellas (eds) (1889–98) **Fasti academiae Mariscallanae Aberdonensis, 1593–1860**
http://www.archive.org/details/fastiacademiaemao1univuoft (vol. 1) http://www.archive.org/details/fastiacademiaemao2univuoft (vol. 2) http://www.archive.org/details/fastiacademiaemao3univuoft (vol. 3)

Armet, Helen (ed.) (1951) **Register of the burgesses of the Burgh of the Canongate:** from 27 June 1622 to 25 September 1733
http://www.archive.org/details/scottishrecordso55scotuoft

Ayrshire roots
http://www.ayrshire-roots.com

Ayrshire towns in Pigot's directory 1837
http://fp.ayrshireroots.plus.com/Genealogy

BMD index
http://www.bmdindex.co.uk

BMD registers
http://bmdregisters.co.uk

British Army WWI Pension records
  http://search.ancestry.co.uk/iexec/Default.
    aspx?htx=List&dbid=1114

Castle Garden
  http://www.castlegarden.org

Census of Ireland 1911
  http://www.census.nationalarchives.ie

Commonwealth War Graves Commission
  http://www.cwgc.org

Convict transportation registers database
  http://www.slq.qld.gov.au/info/fh/convicts

Deceased online
  http://www.deceasedonline.com

Edinburgh University Library: Information services (2008),
Laureations and degrees (1587–1809)
  http://www.archives.lib.ed.ac.uk

Ellis Island
  http://www.ellisisland.org

Evening Times roll of honour
  http://www.glasgow.gov.uk/en/Residents/Library_Services/
    Family_Local_History/eveningtimesrollofhonour.htm

FamilySearch
  http://www.familysearch.org/

Fasti Ecclesiae Scoticanae Vols 1–8
  http://www.archive.org/details/fastiecclesiaescøøscot

Findmypast.com
  http://www.findmypast.com/home.jsp

First World War medal index cards
  http://www.nationalarchives.gov.uk/documentsonline/medals.asp

FreeBMD
  http://freebmd.rootsweb.com

FreeCEN
  http://freecen.rootsweb.com

FreeREG
  http://freereg.rootsweb.com

Glasgow Street Directory 1787
   http://fp.ayrshireroots.plus.com/Genealogy/Historical/Jones%20
      Directory.htm

Grant, Francis J. (ed.) (1906) **Register of apprentices of the city of
Edinburgh, 1583–1666**
   http://www.archive.org/details/registerofappren35edin

Griffith's valuation
   http://griffiths.askaboutireland.ie/gv4/gv_start.php

Henderson, John Alexander (1912) **History of the Society of
Advocates in Aberdeen** (Includes a list of members 1549–1911 with
biographical notes)
   http://www.archive.org/details/historyofsocietyoohendrich

History from headstones
   http://www.historyfromheadstones.com

**History of the Society of Writers to her Majesty's Signet . . . with
list of members . . . from 1594 to 1890 (1890)**
   http://www.archive.org/details/historyofsocietyoosociuoft

**Index to unassisted inward passenger lists to Victoria (Australia)
1852–1923**
   http://proarchives.imagineering.com.au

Ireland, civil registration indexes, 1845–1958
   http://pilot.familysearch.org/recordsearch/start.html#p=
      collectionDetails;t=searchable;c=1408347

Johnston, William (ed.) (1906) **Roll of the graduates of the
University of Aberdeen, 1860–1900**
   http://www.archive.org/details/rollofgraduatesooounivuoft

Military-Genealogy.com
   http://www.military-genealogy.com

Millar, A. H. (1887) **Roll of eminent burgesses of Dundee,
1513–1886**
   http://www.archive.org/details/rollofeminentburoomill

Mills Archive
   http://www.millsarchive.com

Origins Network
   http://www.origins.net

Public Record Office of Northern Ireland: Freeholders' records
http://www.proni.gov.uk/index/search_the_archives/
freeholders_records.htm

Public Record Office of Northern Ireland: Name search (includes
index to pre-1858 wills)
http://www.proni.gov.uk/index/search_the_archives/
proninames.htm

Public Record Office of Northern Ireland: Will calendars
http://www.proni.gov.uk/index/search_the_archives/will_
calendars.htm

ScotlandsPeople
http://www.scotlandspeople.gov.uk/

Scottish ministers
http://www.dwalker.pwp.blueyonder.co.uk/Map.htm

Small, Robert (1904) **History of the congregations of the United
Presbyterian Church from 1733–1900**
http://www.archive.org/details/historyofpresbyto1smaluoft
(vol. 1) http://www.archive.org/details/historyofcongreo2s-
maluoft (vol. 2)

Sugar refiners and sugar bakers database
http://www.mawer.clara.net/intro.html

UK BMD
http://www.ukbmd.org.uk

Ulster Covenant
http://www.proni.gov.uk/index/search_the_archives/ulster_
covenant.htm

**Ulster Historical Foundation: Birth, marriage and death
records**
http://www.ancestryireland.com/database.php

University of Glasgow story: University alumni
http://www.universitystory.gla.ac.uk/alumni

**University of Manchester, John Rylands University Library,
Methodist collections**
http://www.library.manchester.ac.uk/specialcollections/
collections/methodist/

World War Two medals issued to merchant seamen
http://www.nationalarchives.gov.uk/documentsonline/
seamens-medals.asp

PRESENTATION

Crawfurd of Jordanhill family tree
http://www.strath.ac.uk/archives/cat/jhill/crawfurdtree.html

Timperley of Hintlesham
http://personal.strath.ac.uk/g.s.holton/timp

SEARCH ENGINES/DIRECTORIES

Dogpile metacrawler
http://www.dogpile.com/index.gsp

Google
http://www.google.co.uk/

Ixquick metacrawler
http://www.ixquick.com/

Search Engine Watch
http://searchenginewatch.com/

Yahoo
http://www.yahoo.com

SOCIETIES AND ASSOCIATIONS

Aberdeen and North East Scotland Family History Society
http://www.anesfhs.org.uk

Alloway and Southern Ayrshire Family History Society
http://www.asafhs.co.uk

Anglo Scottish Family History Society
http://www.mlfhs.org.uk/AngloScots

Association of Scottish Genealogists and Researchers in Archives (ASGRA)
http://www.asgra.co.uk/

Borders Family History Society
http://www.bordersfhs.org.uk

Caithness Family History Society
http://www.caithnessfhs.org.uk

Catholic Family History Society
http://www.feefhs.org

Central Scotland Family History Society
http://www.csfhs.org.uk

Dumfries and Galloway Family History Society
http://www.dgfhs.org.uk

East Ayrshire Family History Society
http://www.eastayrshirefhs.org.uk

Federation of Family History Societies
http://www.ffhs.org.uk

Fife Family History Society
http://www.fifefhs.org

Glasgow and West of Scotland Family History Society
http://www.gwsfhs.org.uk

Guild of One Name Studies
http://www.one-name.org

Highland Family History Society
http://www.highlandfhs.org.uk

Jewish Genealogical Society of Great Britain
http://www.jgsgb.org.uk

Lanarkshire Family History Society
http://www.lanarkshirefhs.org.uk

Largs and North Ayrshire Family History Society
http://www.largsnafhs.org.uk

Lothians Family History Society
http://www.lothiansfhs.org.uk

Orkney Family History Society
http://www.orkneyfhs.co.uk

Renfrewshire Family History Society
http://www.renfrewshirefhs.co.uk

Scottish Association of Family History Societies
http://www.safhs.org.uk

Scottish Clan and Family Associations
http://clan-maccallum-malcolm.3acres.org/ScotClanFamily.html

Scottish Genealogy Society
http://www.scotsgenealogy.com

Shetland Family History Society
http://www.shetland-fhs.org.uk

Society of Genealogists
http://www.sog.org.uk/index.shtml

Tay Valley Family History Society
http://www.tayvalleyfhs.org.uk

Troon @ Ayrshire Family History Society
http://www.troonayrshirefhs.org.uk

West Lothian Family History Society
http://www.wlfhs.org.uk

SOURCE GUIDES

General Register Office for Scotland: family records
http://www.gro-scotland.gov.uk/famrec/index.html

GENUKI
http://www.genuki.org.uk

Irish ancestors
http://www.irishtimes.com/ancestor

National Archives: research guides
http://www.nationalarchives.gov.uk/gettingstarted/guides.
htm?source=ddmenu_research1

National Archives of Scotland: guides
http://www.nas.gov.uk/guides/default.asp

Scottish Archive Network: research tools
http://www.scan.org.uk/researchrtools/index.htm

SURNAME LISTS

Cyndi's List – surnames: mailing lists
http://www.cyndislist.com/surn-gen.htm#Mailing

GenForum – surnames
http://genforum.genealogy.com/surnames

GENUKI surname lists
http://www.genuki.org.uk/indexes/SurnamesLists.html

RootsWeb Surname List (RSL)
http://rsl.rootsweb.ancestry.com

APPENDIX 4

USEFUL ADDRESSES

NATIONAL RECORDS

Court of the Lord Lyon
New Register House
Edinburgh EH1 3YT
Tel. 0131 556 7255

General Register Office for Scotland
New Register House
Edinburgh EH1 3YT
Tel. 0131 334 0380

National Archives of Scotland
HM General Register House
Edinburgh EH1 3YY
Tel. 0131 535 1314

National Library of Scotland
George IV Bridge
Edinburgh EH1 1EW
Tel. 0131 623 3700

National Register of Archives for Scotland
HM General Register House
Edinburgh EH1 3YY
Tel. 0131 535 1405

Registers of Scotland
Customer Service Centres
Erskine House
68 Queen Street
Edinburgh EH2 4NF
Tel. 0845 607 0161

9 George Square
Glasgow G2 1DY
Tel. 0845 607 0164

Registrar of Births, Deaths and Marriages
89 Commercial Street
Dundee DD1 2AF
Tel. 01382 435222

Scottish Jewish Archives Centre
129 Hill Street
Glasgow G3 6UB
Tel. 0141 332 4911

Strathclyde Area Genealogy Centre
22 Park Circus
Glasgow G3 6BE
Tel. 0141 287 8364

West Register House
Charlotte Square
Edinburgh EH2 4DP

CHURCH OF JESUS CHRIST OF LATTER-DAY SAINTS FAMILY HISTORY CENTRES

Aberdeen
North Anderson Drive
Aberdeen
Tel. 01224 692206

Alloa
Grange Road
Westend Park
Alloa
Tel. 01259 211148

Ayr
Corner of Orchard Avenue and Mossgiel Road
Ayr
Tel. 01292 610632

Dumfries
36 Edinburgh Road
Albanybank
Dumfries
Tel. 01387 254865

Dundee
Bingham Terrace
Dundee
Tel. 01382 451247

Edinburgh
30A Colinton Road
Edinburgh
Tel. 0131 313 2762

Elgin
Pansport Road
Elgin
Tel. 01343 546429

Glasgow
35 Julian Avenue
Glasgow
Tel. 0141 357 1024

Invergordon
Kilmonivaig
Seafield
Portmahomack
Tain
Tel. 01862 871631

Inverness
13 Ness Walk
Inverness
Tel. 01463 231220

Kirkcaldy
Winifred Crescent
Forth Park
Kirkcaldy
Tel. 01592 640041

Lerwick
44 Prince Alfred Street
Lerwick
Tel. 01595 695732

Montrose
Coronation Way
Montrose
Tel. 01674 675753

Motherwell
444–78 Orbiston Street
Motherwell
Tel. 01698 266630

Paisley
Glenburn Road
Paisley
Renfrewshire
Tel. 0141 884 2780

Stornoway
Newton Street
Stornoway
Tel. 01851 870972

LOCAL COLLECTIONS

Aberdeen City Council and Aberdeenshire Council
Aberdeen City Archives
Town House
Broad Street
Aberdeen AB10 1AQ
Tel. 01224 522513

Old Aberdeen House
Dunbar Street
Aberdeen AB22 8YP
Tel. 01224 481775

Angus Council
Angus Archives
Hunter Library
Restenneth Priory
by Forfar DD8 2SZ
Tel. 01307 468644

Argyll and Bute Council
Argyll and Bute Council Archives
Manse Brae
Lochgilphead
Argyll PA31 8QU
Tel. 01546 604120

Ayrshire Councils
Ayrshire Archives Centre
Craigie Estate
Ayr KA8 0SS
Tel. 01292 287584

Borders Council
Scottish Borders Archive and Local History Centre
Heritage Hub
Heart of Hawick
Kirkstile
Hawick TD9 0AE
Tel. 01450 360680

Clackmannanshire Council
Clackmannanshire Council Archives
Library Services
26–8 Drysdale Street
Alloa FK10 1JL
Tel. 01259 722262

Dumfries and Galloway Council
Dumfries and Galloway Archives
33 Burns Street
Dumfries DG1 2PS
Tel. 01387 269254

Dundee City Council
Dundee City Archive and Record Centre
Support Services
21 City Square
Dundee DD1 3BY
Tel. 01382 434494

Search Room
1 Shore Terrace
Dundee
Tel. 01382 434494

East Dunbartonshire Council
East Dunbartonshire Archives
William Patrick Library
2–4 West High Street
Kirkintilloch G66 1AD
Tel. 0141 775 4541

Edinburgh City Council
Edinburgh City Archives
City Chambers
High Street
Edinburgh EH1 1YJ
Tel. 0131 529 4616

Edinburgh Room
Edinburgh City Libraries
Central Library
George IV Bridge
Edinburgh EH1 1EG
Tel. 0131 225 5584

Falkirk Council
Falkirk Archives
Callendar House Museum and History Research Centre
Falkirk FK1 1YR
Tel. 01324 503779

Fife Council
Fife Council Archive Centre
Carleton House
Balgonie Road
Markinch
Fife KY7 6AH
Tel. 01592 413256

Glasgow Archdiocese (Roman Catholic)
Archdiocesan Archive
Archdiocese of Glasgow Curial Offices
196 Clyde Street
Glasgow G1 4JY
Tel. 0141 226 5898 ext. 154

Glasgow City Council
Glasgow City Archives
Mitchell Library
201 North Street
Glasgow G3 7DN
Tel. 0141 287 2910

History and Glasgow Room
Mitchell Library
201 North Street
Glasgow G3 7DN
Tel. 0141 287 2937

Highland Council
Highland Council Archive Service and Registration Centre
Bught Road
Inverness IV3 5SS
Tel. 01463 256444

Lochaber Archive Centre
Lochaber College
An Aird
Fort William PH33 6AN
Tel. 01397 701942

North Highland Archive
Wick Library
Sinclair Terrace
Wick KW1 5AB
Tel. 01955 606432

Midlothian Council
Midlothian Council Archives
Library Headquarters
2 Clerk Street
Loanhead EH20 9DR
Tel. 0131 440 2210

Moray Council
Local Heritage Centre
East End School
Institution Road
Elgin IV30 1RP
Tel. 01343 569011

North Lanarkshire Council
North Lanarkshire Archives
10 Kelvin Road
Lenziemill G67 2BA
Tel. 01236 638980

Orkney Council
Orkney Archives
Orkney Library and Archive
44 Junction Road
Kirkwall KW15 1AG
Tel. 01856 873166

Perth and Kinross Council
Perth and Kinross Council Archive
A. K. Bell Library
2–8 York Place
Perth PH2 8EP
Tel. 01738 477012

Shetland Council
Shetland Archives
Shetland Museum and Archives
Hay's Dock
Lerwick ZE1 0WP
Tel. 01595 695057

South Lanarkshire Council
South Lanarkshire Archives
Records Management Unit
30 Hawbank Road
College Milton
East Kilbride G74 5EX
Tel. 01355 239193

Stirling Council
Stirling Council Archives Services
5 Borrowmeadow Road
Stirling FK7 7UW
Tel. 01786 450745

West Lothian Council
West Lothian Council
Archives and Records Centre
9 Dunlop Square
Deans Industrial Estate
Livingston EH54 8SB
Tel. 01506 773770

MEDICAL RECORDS

Dumfries and Galloway Health Board Archives
Easterbrook Hall
Crichton Royal Hospital
Dumfries DG1 4TG
Tel. 01387 255301

Lothian Health Services Archive
University of Edinburgh Library
George Square
Edinburgh EH8 9LJ
Tel. 0131 650 3392

NHS Greater Glasgow and Clyde Board Archive
University of Glasgow
13 Thurso Street
Glasgow G11 6PE
Tel. 0141 330 5515

Northern Health Services Archives
Aberdeen Royal Infirmary
Woolmanhill
Aberdeen AB1 1LD
Tel. 01224 663456 ext. 55562; 01224 663123

Royal College of Physicians and Surgeons of Glasgow
232–42 St Vincent Street
Glasgow G2 5RJ
Tel. 0141 221 6072

Royal College of Physicians of Edinburgh
9 Queen Street
Edinburgh EH2 1JQ
Tel. 0131 225 7324

Royal College of Surgeons of Edinburgh
18 Nicolson Street
Edinburgh EH8 9DW
Tel. 0131 527 1630

OCCUPATIONAL RECORDS

Advocates Library
Parliament House
Edinburgh EH1 1RF
Tel. 0131 226 5071

HBOS plc Group Archives
12 Bankhead Crossway South
Sighthill
Edinburgh EH11 4EN
Tel. 0131 529 1307

Royal Bank of Scotland Group Archives
6 South Gyle Crescent Lane
Edinburgh EH12 9EG
Fax. 0131 334 2270

Signet Library
Parliament Square
Edinburgh EH1 1RF
Tel. 0131 220 3249

University of Glasgow Archive Services
13 Thurso Street
Glasgow G11 6PE
Tel. 0141 330 5515

ENGLISH RECORDS

General Register Office for England and Wales
PO Box 2
Southport PR8 2JD
Tel. 0151 471 4800

Principal Registry of the Family Division
First Avenue House
42–9 High Holborn
London WC1V 6NP
Tel. 020 7947 6000

National Archives
Ruskin Avenue
Kew
Richmond TW9 4DU
Tel. 020 8876 3444

IRISH RECORDS

REPUBLIC OF IRELAND

The General Register Office
Government Offices
Convent Road
Roscommon
Tel. +353 (0) 90 663 2900

National Archives of Ireland
Bishop Street
Dublin 8
Tel. + 353 (0) 1 407 2300

National Library of Ireland
Kildare Street
Dublin 2
Tel. +353 (0) 1 603 0200

Office of the Chief Herald of Ireland
Kildare Street
Dublin 2
Tel. +353 (0) 1 603 0200

Registry of Deeds
Kings Inns
Henrietta Street
Dublin 7
Tel. +353 (0) 1 670 7500

NORTHERN IRELAND

General Register Office (Northern Ireland)
Oxford House
49–55 Chichester Street
Belfast BT1 4HL
Tel. 028 9025 2000

Presbyterian Historical Society
Room 218
Church House
Fisherwick Place
Belfast BT1 6DW
Tel. 028 9032 2284

Public Record Office of Northern Ireland
66 Balmoral Avenue
Belfast BT9 6NY
Tel. 028 9025 5905

SOCIETIES AND ASSOCIATIONS

Aberdeen and North East Scotland Family History Society
The Hon. Secretary
The Family History Shop
164 King Street
Aberdeen AB24 5BD
Tel. 01224 646323

Alloway and Southern Ayrshire Family History Society
Alloway Parish Church Hall
Auld Nick's View
Alloway
Ayr KA7 4RT

Anglo Scottish Family History Society
The Hon. Secretary
c/o Manchester and Lancashire Family History Society
Clayton House
59 Piccadilly
Manchester M1 2AQ
Tel. 0161 236 9750

Borders Family History Society
The Hon. Membership Secretary
35 Corbar Road
Stockport
Cheshire SK2 6EP

Caithness Family History Society
Secretary
9 Provost Cormack Drive
Thurso KW14 7ES

Catholic Family History Society
Membership Secretary
14 Sydney Road
Ilford IG6 2ED

Central Scotland Family History Society
Secretary
11 Springbank Gardens
Dunblane FK15 9JX

Dumfries and Galloway Family History Society
Family History Centre
9 Glasgow Street
Dumfries DG2 9AF
Tel. 01387 248093

East Ayrshire Family History Society
c/o Dick Institute
Elmbank Avenue
Kilmarnock KA1 3BU

Federation of Family History Societies
PO Box 8857
Lutterworth LE17 9BJ

Fife Family History Society
Secretary
'Glenmoriston'
Durie Street
Leven KY8 4HF

Glasgow and West of Scotland Family History Society
Unit 13, 32 Mansfield Street
Glasgow G11 5QP
Tel. 0141 339 8303

Guild of One Name Studies
The Secretary
Box G
14 Charterhouse Buildings
Goswell Road
London EC1M 7BA

Highland Family History Society
The Secretary
14 Leachkin Avenue
Inverness IV3 8LH

Jewish Genealogical Society of Great Britain
33 Seymour Place
London W1H 5AU
Tel. 020 7724 4232

Lanarkshire Family History Society
Unit 26A, Motherwell Business Centre
Coursington Road
Motherwell
Lanarkshire ML1 1PW

Largs and North Ayrshire Family History Society
The Secretary
c/o Largs Library
26 Allanpark Street
Largs KA30 9AG

Lothians Family History Society
Lasswade High School Centre
Eskdale Drive
Bonnyrigg
Midlothian EH19 2LA

Milngavie Family History Society
Milngavie Community Education Centre
Allander Road
Milngavie
Glasgow G62 8PN
Tel. 0141 956 1566

Orkney Family History Society
Orkney Library and Archives
44 Junction Road
Kirkwall
Orkney KW15 1AG

Renfrewshire Family History Society
Membership Secretary
c/o 51 Mathie Crescent
Gourock
Scotland PA19 1YU

Scottish Genealogy Society
Library and Family History Centre
15 Victoria Terrace
Edinburgh EH1 2JL
Tel. 0131 220 3677

Shetland Family History Society
6 Hillhead
Lerwick
Shetland ZE1 0EJ

Society of Genealogists
14 Charterhouse Buildings
Goswell Road
London EC1M 7BA
Tel. 020 7251 8799

Tay Valley Family History Society
The Hon. Secretary
Family History Research Centre
179–81 Princes Street
Dundee DD4 6DQ
Tel. 01382 461845

Troon @ Ayrshire Family History Society
c/o MERC
Troon Public Library
South Beach
Troon KA10 6AF

West Lothian Family History Society
23 Templar Rise
Livingston EH54 6PJ

APPENDIX 5

SAMPLE FORMS FOR OBTAINING AND RECORDING INFORMATION

Family questionnaire form

FAMILY QUESTIONNAIRE FORM

(Please give full names and previous surname(s) where appropriate)

	You	Your **Husband/Wife** (& maiden name)
Name	....	....
Date & Place of Birth/Baptism	....	....
Date & Place of Marriage	....	....
Date & Place of Death/Burial	....	....
Occupation	....	....

Your Children

	1	2	3 ....

Name	....
Date & Place of Birth/Baptism	....
Date & Place of Marriage	....
Name of Husband/Wife	....
Date & Place of Death/Burial	....
Occupation	....
Their Children	1 ....
	2 ....
	3 ....

Your Father

Name ....

Date & Place of Birth/Baptism ....

Date & Place of Marriage ....

Date & Place of Death/Burial ....

Occupation ....

Your FATHER'S Father

Name ....

Date & Place of Birth/Baptism ....

Date & Place of Marriage ....

Date & Place of Death/Burial ....

Occupation ....

Your MOTHER'S Father

Name ....

Date & Place of Birth/Baptism ....

Date & Place of Marriage ....

Date & Place of Death/Burial ....

Occupation ....

Your current address ....
....
....

Telephone number ....

Your Mother (& maiden name)
....
....
....
....

His Wife (& maiden name)
....
....
....
....

His Wife (& maiden name)
....
....
....
....

Other Family Members

Do you know any other information about other relatives, such as uncles, aunts, great-uncles, great-aunts, cousins?

1. Full Name .... Relationship.........................
   Details ....
   ....
   ....
   ....

2. Full Name .... Relationship.........................
   Details ....
   ....
   ....
   ....

3. Full Name .... Relationship.........................
   Details ....
   ....
   ....
   ....

Family Traditions

Are there any family traditions or stories which you can recall?

....
....
....
....
....
....
....
....
....
....
....
....
....
....

Do you know of the existence of a family Bible? Does it have family details? Where is it?

....
....
....
....

Form for recording birth certificate details

Birth Certificate Details

First Names:

Surname:

When:

Where:

Father's Name:

Father's Occupation:

Mother's Name:

Date of Marriage (except 1856–60):

Informant:

   Qualification:

   Residence:

When Registered:

Where Registered:

Registrar:

Birth Certificate Details

First Names:

Surname:

When:

Where:

Father's Name:

Father's Occupation:

Mother's Name:

Date of Marriage (except 1856–60):

Informant:

   Qualification:

   Residence:

When Registered:

Where Registered:

Registrar:

Form for recording marriage certificate details

Marriage Certificate Details

When, where and how:

Name of GROOM:
    Status:
    Occupation:
    Age:
    Usual Residence:

Name of BRIDE:
    Status:
    Occupation:
    Age:
    Usual Residence:

Father of GROOM:
    Occupation:
    Mother:

Father of BRIDE:
    Occupation:
    Mother:

Minister/Registrar:
When & Where:

Witnesses:

Marriage Certificate Details

When, where and how:

Name of GROOM:
    Status:
    Occupation:
    Age:
    Usual Residence:

Name of BRIDE:
    Status:
    Occupation:
    Age:
    Usual Residence:

Father of GROOM:
    Occupation:
    Mother:

Father of BRIDE:
    Occupation:
    Mother:

Minister/Registrar:
When & Where:

Witnesses:

Form for recording death certificate details

Death Certificate Details

Name:
    Occupation:
    Status:

When:

Where:

Age:

Father's Name:
    Occupation:

Mother's Name
    Maiden Name

Cause of Death
    Duration of Disease:
    Physician:

Informant's Name:
    Qualification:
    Residence:

When Registered:
    Where:
    Registrar

Death Certificate Details

Name:
    Occupation:
    Status:

When:

Where:

Age:

Father's Name:
    Occupation:

Mother's Name
    Maiden Name

Cause of Death
    Duration of Disease:
    Physician:

Informant's Name:
    Qualification:
    Residence:

When Registered:
    Where:
    Registrar

Form for recording census return details

Year   Parish   County   Enumerator

Address	Name	Reln	M or S	Age	Occupation	Where Born

Form for recording IGI details

IGI Details

Person 1	Person 2	Person 3	Sex	Type	Date	Parish

BIBLIOGRAPHY

GENERAL

Adolph, Anthony (2008), *Collins tracing your Scottish family history*, London: Collins.

Bigwood, Rosemary (1998), *Index to parishes: With related sheriff courts, commissary courts, and burghs* [Scotland].

Bigwood, Rosemary (2006), *The Scottish family tree detective: Tracing your ancestors in Scotland*, Manchester: Manchester University Press.

Blatchford, Robert and Blatchford, Elizabeth (eds) (2008), *The family and local history handbook, 11*, York: Robert Blatchford Publishing.

Burness, Lawrence R. (1991), *A Scottish genealogist's glossary*, Aberdeen: Scottish Association of Family History Societies.

Cairns-Smith-Barth and Lawrence, John (1986), *Scottish family history: A research and source guide with particular emphasis on how to do your research from various sources available within Australia*, vol. 1. Hampton Vic.: Sue E. MacBeth Genealogical Books.

Christmas, Brian (1991), *Sources for one-name studies and for other family historians: A selected list and finding aid*, London: Guild of One-Name Studies.

Cole, Jean and Titford, John (2003), *Tracing your family tree: The comprehensive guide to discovering your family history*, 4th ed., Newbury: Countryside Books.

Colwell, Stella (2007), *Teach yourself tracing your family history*, 3rd ed., London: Teach Yourself.

Cory, Kathleen B. (2004), *Tracing your Scottish ancestry*, 3rd ed., Edinburgh: Polygon.

Diack, H. Lesley (2008), *North east roots: A guide to sources*, 5th ed., Aberdeen: Aberdeen and NE Scotland Family History Society.

Drake, Michael (ed.) (1994), *Time, family and community: Perspectives on family and community history*, Oxford: Blackwell in association with The Open University.

Drake, Michael and Finnegan, Ruth (eds) (1997), *Sources and methods for family and community historians: A handbook*, 2nd rev. ed., Cambridge: Cambridge University Press in association with The Open University. (*Studying family and community history: 19th and 20th centuries* : vol. 4.)

Dumfries and Galloway: Some sources and places of interest for local and family history (1995), Dumfries: Dumfries and Galloway Family History Society.

Durie, Bruce (2009), *Scottish genealogy*, Stroud: History Press.

Finnegan, Ruth and Drake, Michael (eds) (1994), *From family tree to family history*, Cambridge: Cambridge University Press in association with The Open University. (*Studying family and community history: 19th and 20th centuries*: vol. 1.)

FitzHugh, Terrick V. H. (1998), *The dictionary of genealogy*, 5th ed., rev. by Susan Lumas, London: A. and C. Black.

Fowler, Simon (2001), *Tracing Scottish ancestors*, Richmond: Public Record Office.

Gandy, Michael (1993), *An introduction to planning research: Shortcuts in family history*, Birmingham: Federation of Family History Societies.

Golby, John (ed.) (1994), *Communities and families*, Cambridge: Cambridge University Press in association with The Open University, 1994. (*Studying family and community history: 19th and 20th centuries*: vol. 3.)

Hamilton-Edwards, Gerald (1983a), *In search of ancestry*, 4th ed., Chichester: Phillimore.

Hamilton-Edwards, Gerald (1983b), *In search of Scottish ancestry*, 2nd rev. ed., Chichester: Phillimore.

Herber, Mark D. (2004), *Ancestral trails: The complete guide to British genealogy and family history*, 2nd ed., Stroud: Sutton.

Hey, David (ed.) (2008), *The Oxford companion to family and local history*, 2nd ed., Oxford: Oxford University Press.

Irvine, Sherry (2003), *Your Scottish ancestry*, 2nd rev. ed., Salt Lake City: Ancestry.

James, Alwyn (2002), *Scottish roots: The step-by-step guide to tracing your ancestors*, new rev. ed., Edinburgh: Luath Press, 2002.

Kennedy, Ian, Ruthven, Louise and McCulloch, Jean (eds) (2001), *Sources for family history in Ayrshire*, rev. ed. [Troon]: Troon@Ayrshire Family History Society.

Miller, Susan (1995), *Strathclyde sources: A guide for family historians*, 2nd ed., Glasgow: Glasgow and West of Scotland Family History Society.

Mills, Elizabeth Shown (2007), *Evidence explained: citing history sources from artifacts to cyberspace*, Baltimore: Genealogical Publishing Co.

Moody, David (1994), *Scottish family history*, Baltimore: Genealogical Publishing Co.

National Archives of Scotland (2009), *Tracing your Scottish ancestors: The official guide*, 5th ed., Edinburgh: Birlinn.

Practice makes perfect: A workbook of genealogical exercises (1993), Birmingham: Federation of Family History Societies.

Pryce, W. T. R. (ed.) (1994), *From family history to community history*, Cambridge: Cambridge University Press in association with The Open University. (*Studying family and community history: 19th and 20th centuries*: vol. 2)

Sandison, Alexander (1985), *Tracing ancestors in Shetland*, 3rd ed., London: A. Sandison.

Saul, Pauline (2002), *The family historians enquire within*, 6th ed., Bury: Federation of Family History Societies.

Steel, D. J. (ed.) (1970), *National index of parish register*, vol. 12: *Sources for Scottish genealogy and family history*, London: Phillimore.

Tay Valley Family History Society source book (1988), Dundee: Tay Valley Family History Society.

Todd, Andrew (2000), *Nuts and bolts: Family history problem solving through family reconsitution techniques*, 2nd ed., Bury: Allen and Todd.

Wheeler, Meg (2000), *Tracing your roots: Locating your ancestors at home and abroad*, New York: Todtri.

ARCHIVES AND RECORD OFFICES

Bevan, Amanda (2006), *Tracing your ancestors in The National Archives: The Website and beyond*, 7th rev. ed., Kew: The National Archives.

Cole, Jean and Church, Rosemary (1998), *In and around record repositories in Great Britain and Ireland*, 4th ed., Ramsey, Huntingdon: Armstrong, Boon, Marriott Publishing.

Foster, Janet and Sheppard, Julia (2002), *British archives: A guide to archive resources in the United Kingdom*, 4th ed., London: Palgrave.

Gibson, Jeremy and Peskett, Pamela (2002), *Record offices: How to find them*, 9th ed., Bury: Federation of Family History Societies.

Livingstone, M. (1905), *A guide to the public records of Scotland deposited in H. M. General Register House, Edinburgh*, Edinburgh: H. M. General Register House.

Mortimer, Ian (ed.) (1999), *Record repositories in Great Britain*, 11th ed., London: Public Record Office.

Scottish Record Office (1996), *Guide to the national archives of Scotland*, Edinburgh: The Stationery Office.

Thomson, J. Maitland (1922), *The public records of Scotland*, Glasgow: Maclehose, Jackson and Co.

Wood, Tom (1999), *Using record offices for family historians*, 2nd ed. Bury: Federation of Family History Societies.

BACKGROUND INFORMATION

Burness, Lawrence R. (1997), *A Scottish historian's glossary*, Aberdeen: Scottish Association of Family History Societies.

Chapman, Colin R. (1995), *How heavy, how much and how long? Weights, money and other measures used by our ancestors*, Dursley: Lochin Publishing.

Cheney, C. R. (ed.) (2008), *A handbook of dates for students of British history*, 2nd ed. revised by Michael Jones, Cambridge: Cambridge University Press.

Cox, Michael (1999), *Exploring Scottish history: With a directory of resource centres for Scottish local and national history in Scotland*, 2nd ed., Hamilton: Scottish Library Association.

Gouldesbrough, Peter (1985), *Formulary of old Scots legal documents*, Edinburgh: Stair Society.

Groome, Francis H. (ed.) [1903] (1998), 6 vols, *Ordnance gazetteer of Scotland*, Bristol: Thoemmes Press.

Index of Scottish place names (1990), 1981 ed. Edinburgh: HMSO.

Mitchell, B. R. (1988), *British historical statistics*, Cambridge: Cambridge University Press.

Munby, Lionel (1996), *How much is that worth?*, 2nd ed., Chichester: Phillimore.

New statistical account of Scotland (1845) (15 vols), Edinburgh: W. Blackwood and Sons. Available online. See List of Websites.

O'Rourke, Stephen Robb-Russell (2009), *Glossary of legal terms*, 5th rev. ed. Edinburgh: W. Green.

Statistical account of Scotland (1791–99) (21 vols), Edinburgh: W. Creech. Available online. See List of Websites.

Steinberg, S. H. (1991), *Historical tables, 58 BC–AD 1990*, 12th ed., London: Palgrave.

Third statistical account of Scotland (1951–92), (various publishers).

Torrance, D. Richard (1996), *Weights and measures for the Scottish family historian*, Aberdeen: Scottish Association of Family History Societies.

BIBLIOGRAPHIES

Hancock, P. D. (1959) (2 vols), *A bibliography of works relating to Scotland 1916–1950*, Edinburgh: Edinburgh University Press.

Mitchell, Sir Arthur and Cash, C. G. (1917) (2 vols), *A contribution to the bibliography of Scottish topography*, Edinburgh: Scottish History Society.

Moore, Marjorie (1996), *Sources for Scottish genealogy in the library of the Society of Genealogists*, London: Society of Genealogists.

National Library of Scotland (1978–88), *Bibliography of Scotland 1976–1987*, Edinburgh: National Library of Scotland. (1988– online).

Raymond, Stuart A. (1991–4) (4 vols), *British genealogical periodicals: A bibliography of their contents*, Birmingham: Federation of Family History Societies; Exeter: S. A. and M. J. Raymond.

BIOGRAPHICAL DICTIONARIES

Anderson, William (1875), *The Scottish Nation*, Edinburgh: A. Fullarton.

Boase, Frederic (1892–1921) (6 vols), *Modern English biography*, Truro: Netherton and Worth.

British biographical archive 'on microfiche' (1984, 1991), London: K. G. Saur.

Brown, James D. and Stratton, Stephen Samuel (1897), *British musical biography*, Birmingham: Chadfield.

Chambers, Robert (1835 and later editions), *A biographical dictionary of eminent Scotsmen*, London: Blackie.

Ewan, E., Innes, S., Reynolds, S. and Pipes, R. (eds) (2006), *The biographical dictionary of Scottish women*, Edinburgh: Edinburg University Press.

Eyre-Todd, George (1909), *Who's who in Glasgow in 1909*, Glasgow: Gowans and Gray (available online).

Goring, Rosemary (ed.) (1992), *Chambers Scottish biographical dictionary*, London: Chambers.

Jeremy, D. and Shaw, C. (eds) (1984-6) (5 vols and supplement), *Dictionary of business biography*, London: Butterworth.

Oxford Dictionary of National Biography (2004) (61 vols), Oxford: Oxford University Press (available online).

Saville, J. and Bellamy, J. (1992) (9 vols), *Dictionary of labour biography*, London: Macmillan.

Slaven, Anthony and Checkland, Sydney (eds) (1986, 1990) (2 vols), *Dictionary of Scottish business biography, 1860-1960*, Aberdeen: Aberdeen University Press.

Who's who (1849–) London: A. and C. Black (Biographical information included from 1897).

Who was who (1897–) London: A. and C. Black (available online)

CENSUS

Christian, Peter and Annal, David (2008), *Census: The expert guide*, Kew: National Archives.

Escott, Anne (1986), *Census returns and old parochial registers on microfilm: A directory of public library holdings in the West of Scotland*, rev. ed., Glasgow: Glasgow District Libraries.

Gibson, Jeremy and Hampson, Elizabeth (2000), *Marriage and census indexes for family historians*, 8th ed., Bury: Federation of Family History Societies.

Gibson, Jeremy and Hampson, Elizabeth (2001), *Census returns 1841–1891 in microform: A directory to local holdings in Great Britain; Channel Islands; Isle of Man*, 6th ed., Bury: Federation of Family History Societies.

Gibson, Jeremy and Medlycott, Mervyn (2001), *Local census listings, 1522–1930: Holdings in the British Isles*, 3rd ed., Bury: Federation of Family History Societies.

Higgs, Edward (2005), *Making sense of the census revisited: Census records for England and Wales, 1801–1901: A handbook for historical researchers*, London: Institute of Historical Research.

Johnson, Gordon (1997), *Census records for Scottish families at home and abroad*, 3rd ed., Aberdeen: Aberdeen and North-East Scotland Family History Society.

Mills, Dennis and Schurer, Kevin (eds) (1996), *Local communities in the Victorian census enumerators' books*, Oxford: Leopard's Head Press.

Ruthven-Murray, Peter (1998), *Scottish census indexes: covering the 1841–1871 civil censuses*, Aberdeen: Scottish Association of Family History Societies.

Sinclair, Cecil (2000), *Jock Tamson's bairns: A history of the records of the General Register Office for Scotland*, Edinburgh: General Register Office for Scotland.

CIVIL REGISTRATION

Sinclair, Cecil (2000), *Jock Tamson's bairns: A history of the records of the General Register Office for Scotland*, Edinburgh: General Register Office for Scotland.

Wood, Tom (2000), *An Introduction to British civil registration*, 2nd ed, Bury: Federation of Family History Societies.

CLANS

Adam, Frank (2005), *The clans, septs and regiments of the Scottish Highlands*, 8th ed., revised by Sir Thomas Innes of Learney, Doune: Clan Book Sales.

Martine, Roddy (2004), *Scottish clan and family names: Their arms, origins and tartans*, new rev. ed., Edinburgh: Mainstream.

COMPUTERS

Christian, Peter (2009), *The genealogist's Internet*, 4th ed., Kew: National Archives.

Crowe, Elizabeth Powell (2008), *Genealogy online*, 8th ed., Emeryville, CA: McGraw-Hill.

Gale, Thornton and Gale, Marty (2007), *Getting started on your genealogy website*, Mercer Island, WA: www.genealogyhosting.com.

Gormley, Myra Vanderpool and Lord, Tana Pedersen (2007), *The official guide to RootsWeb.com*, Provo, UT: Ancestry.

Hendrickson, Nancy (2003), *Finding your roots online*, Cincinnati: Betterway Books.

Kemp, Thomas Jay (2003), *Virtual roots 2.0: A guide to genealogy and local history on the World Wide Web*, 2nd rev. ed., Wilmington, DE: Scholarly Resources.

Kovacs, Diane K. (2002), *Genealogical research on the Web*, New York: Neal-Schuman Publishers.

Lawton, Guy (1994), *Spreadsheet family trees*, London: David Hawgood.

McClure, Rhonda (2002), *The complete idiot's guide to online genealogy*, 2nd ed., Indianapolis: Alpha Books.

McClure, Rhonda R. (2004), *Digitizing your family history: Easy methods for preserving your heirloom documents, photos, home movies and more in a digital format*, Cincinnati: Family Tree Books.

MacRae, Kyle (2005), *Haynes Internet genealogy manual*, Yeovil: Haynes.

Marelli, Diane (2007), *@ home with your ancestors.com: How to research family history using the Internet*, Oxford: How To Books.

Morgan, George G. (2008), *The official guide to Ancestry.com*, 2nd ed., Provo, UT: Ancestry.

Peacock, Caroline (2005), *Good Web guide genealogy: The simple way to explore the Internet*, 4th ed., London: Good Web Guide Ltd.

Raymond, Stuart A. (2008), *Family history on the Web: A directory for England and Wales*, Bury: Federation of Family History Societies in association with S. A. and M. J. Raymond.

Reader's Digest (2008), *How to trace your family history on the Internet*, London: Reader's Digest.

Thomas, Jenny, Helm, Matthew L. and Helm, April Leigh (2007), *Genealogy online for dummies*, Chichester: Wiley.

CURRENT RESEARCH

'Register of one-name studies 2008' (2008), 24th ed., London: Guild of One-Name Studies.

EDUCATION

Chapman, Colin R. (1992), *The growth of British education and its records*, 2nd ed., Dursley: Lochin Publishing.

Chapman, Colin R. (1999), *Basic facts about using education records*, Bury: Federation of Family History Societies.

Craigie, James (1970), *A bibliography of Scottish education before 1872*, London: University of London Press.

Craigie, James (1974), *A bibliography of Scottish education 1872–1972*, London: University of London Press.

Jacobs, Phyllis M. (1964), *Registers of the universities, colleges and schools of Great Britain and Ireland*, London: Athlone Press.

Society of Genealogists (1996), *School, university and college registers and histories in the library of the Society of Genealogists*, 2nd ed., London: Society of Genealogists.

ABERDEEN UNIVERSITY

Anderson, Peter John (ed.) (1893), *Officers and graduates of University and King's College, Aberdeen, 1495–1860*, Aberdeen: New Spalding Club.

Anderson, Peter John (ed.) (1900), *Roll of alumni in Arts of the University and King's College of Aberdeen, 1596–1860*, Aberdeen: University of Aberdeen.

Anderson, Peter John and Johnstone, James Fowler Kellas (eds) (1889–98) (3 vols), *Fasti academiae Mariscallanae Aberdonensis, 1593–1860*, Aberdeen: New Spalding Club (available online).

Donald, L. and Macdonald, W. S. (eds) (1982), *Roll of the graduates of the University of Aberdeen 1956–1970 with supplement 1860–1955*, Aberdeen: Aberdeen University Press.

Johnston, William (ed.) (1906), *Roll of the graduates of the University of Aberdeen, 1860–1900*, Aberdeen: University of Aberdeen (available online).

McDonnell, Frances (1996), *Alumni and graduates in arts of the Aberdeen colleges, 1840–1849*, St Andrews: F. McDonnell.

McDonnell, Frances (1996), *Alumni and graduates in arts of the Aberdeen colleges, 1850–1860*, St Andrews: F. McDonnell

Mackintosh, John (compiler) (1960), *Roll of the graduates of the University of Aberdeen 1926–1955; with supplement 1860–1925*, Aberdeen: University of Aberdeen.

Watt, Theodore (compiler) (1935), *Roll of the graduates of the University of Aberdeen 1901–1925; with supplement 1860–1900*, Aberdeen: Aberdeen University Press.

GLASGOW UNIVERSITY

Addison, W. Innes (compiler) (1898), *A roll of the graduates of the University of Glasgow from 1727 to 1897*, Glasgow: J. Maclehose and Sons (available online).

Addison, W. Innes (ed.) (1913), *The matriculation albums of the University of Glasgow from 1728 to 1858*, Glasgow: J. Maclehose and Sons (available online).

Munimenta Alme Universitatis Glasguensis (1854) (3 vols and index), *Records of the University of Glasgow: From its foundation till 1727*, Glasgow: Maitland Club.

ST ANDREWS UNIVERSITY

Anderson, James Maitland (ed.) (1905), *The matriculation roll of the University of St Andrews, 1747–1897*, Edinburgh: W. Blackwood and Sons.

Anderson, James Maitland (ed.) (1926), *Early records of the University of St Andrews: The graduate roll 1413–1579 and the matriculation roll 1473–1579*, Edinburgh: Scottish History Society.

Dunlop, Annie I. (ed) (1964), *Acta facultatis artium Universitatis Sanctandree, 1413–1588*, Edinburgh: Oliver and Boyd.

Smart, Robert N. (2004), *Biographical register of the University of St Andrews, 1747–1897*, St Andrews: University of St Andrews Library.

EMIGRATION AND IMMIGRATION

Dictionary of Scottish emigrants into England and Wales (1984–92) (5 vols), Manchester: Anglo-Scottish Family History Society, then Manchester and Lancashire Family History Society.

Dobson, David, many publications. For details see http://www.btinternet.com/~lds.dobson/list.html.

Filby, P. William and Meyer, Mary K. (1981–), *Passenger and immigration lists index*, Detroit: Gale Research Co.

Kershaw, Roger (2002), *Emigrants and expats: A guide to sources on UK emigration and residents overseas*, Richmond: Public Record Office.

Kershaw, Roger and Pearsall, Mark (2004), *Immigrants and aliens*, 2nd ed., Kew: National Archives.

Lawson, James (1990), *The emigrant Scots: An inventory of extant ships manifests (passenger lists) in Canadian archives for ships travelling from Scotland to Canada before 1900*, Aberdeen: Aberdeen and North-East Scotland Family History Society.

Num, Cora (1999), *How to find shipping and immigration records in Australia*, 4th ed., Pearce ACT: Cora Num.

Scottish Record Office (1994?), *The peoples of Scotland: A multi-cultural history: Historical background, list of documents, extracts and facsimiles*, Edinburgh: Scottish Record Office.

Whyte, Donald (1972, 1986) (2 vols), *Dictionary of Scottish emigrants to the USA*, Baltimore: Magna Carta Books Co.

Whyte, Donald (1986, 1995) (2 vols), *Dictionary of Scottish emigrants to Canada before Confederation*, Toronto: Ontario Genealogical Society.

Whyte, Donald (1995), *The Scots overseas: a selected bibliography*, new rev. ed., Aberdeen: Scottish Association of Family History Societies.

Wilkins, Frances (1993), *Family histories in Scottish customs records*, Kidderminster: Wyre Forest Press.

Yeo, Geoffrey and White, Philippa (eds) (1995), *The British overseas: a guide to records of their births, baptisms, marriages, deaths and burials, available in the United Kingdom*, 3rd ed. (Guildhall Library research guide 2), London: Guildhall Library.

GENETICS

Daus, Carol (1999), *Past imperfect: How tracing your family medical history can save your life*, Santa Monica, CA: Santa Monica Press.

Gormley, Myra Vanderpool (1998), *Family diseases: Are you at risk?* Baltimore: Clearfield.

Oppenheimer, Stephen (2007), *The origins of the British: A genetic detective story*, London: Robinson.

Pomery, Chris (2007), *Family history in the genes: Trace your DNA and grow your family tree*, Kew: The National Archives.

Robinson, Tara Rodden (2005), *Genetics for dummies*, Hoboken, NJ: Wiley.

Savin, Alan (2000), *DNA for family historians*, Maidenhead: Alan Savin.

Sykes, Bryan (ed.) (1999), *The human inheritance: Genes, language and evolution*, Oxford: Oxford University Press.

Sykes, Bryan (2004), *The seven daughters of Eve*, London: Corgi.

Sykes, Bryan (2007), *Blood of the Isles: Exploring the genetic roots of our tribal history*, London: Corgi.

HANDWRITING

Hector, L. C. [1966] (1980), *The handwriting of English documents*, 2nd ed., Dorking: Kohler and Coombes.

Johnson, Charles and Jenkinson, Hilary (1915) (2 vols), *English court hand, AD 1066 to 1500*, Oxford: Clarendon Press.

Scottish Record Office (1994), *Scottish handwriting 1500–1700: A self-help pack*, [Edinburgh]: Scottish Record Office.

Simpson, Grant G. (1998), *Scottish handwriting 1150–1650: An introduction to the reading of documents*, new ed., East Linton: Tuckwell Press.

HERALDRY

Boutell, Charles (1988), *Boutell's heraldry* (revised by J. P. Brooke-Little). rev. ed., London: Frederick Warne.

Burnett, Charles J. and Dennis, Mark D. (1997), *Scotland's heraldic heritage: The Lion rejoicing*, Edinburgh: The Stationery Office.

Friar, Stephen (1996), *Heraldry for the local historian and genealogist*, Stroud: Sutton.

Innes of Learney, Sir Thomas (1978), *Scots heraldry*, new ed. rev. by Malcolm R. Innes., London: Johnston and Bacon.

Moncrieffe of that Ilk, Sir Iain and Pottinger, Don (1978), *Simple heraldry*, 2nd ed., rev., Edinburgh: Bartholomew.

Paul, Sir James Balfour [1977] (2001), *An ordinary of arms contained in the Public Register of All Arms and Bearings (1672–1902)*, with vol. 2 (1903–73) by David Reid of Robertland and Vivien Wilson, Baltimore: Clearfield.

Swinnerton, Iain (1995), *Basic facts about heraldry for family historians*, Birmingham: Federation of Family History Societies.

HISTORICAL DEMOGRAPHY

Flinn, Michael (ed.) (1977), *Scottish population history from the 17th century to the 1930s*, Cambridge: Cambridge University Press.

Fraser, W. Hamish and Maver, Irene (eds) (1996), *Glasgow, volume II: 1830 to 1912*, Manchester: Manchester University Press.

Hinde, Andrew (1998), *Demographic methods*, London: Arnold.

Macdonald, D. F. (1978), *Scotland's shifting population, 1770–1850*, Philadelphia: Porcupine Press.

Pooley, Colin and Turnbull, Jean (1998), *Migration and mobility in Britain since the eighteenth century*, London: UCL Press.

Schurer, Kevin and Arkell, Tom (eds) (1992), *Surveying the people*, Oxford: Leopard's Head.

Todd, Andrew (2000), *Nuts and bolts: Family history problem solving through family reconstitution techniques*, 2nd ed., Bury: Allen and Todd.

Wrigley, E. A. (Ed.) (1966), *An introduction to English historical demography*, London: Weidenfeld and Nicolson.

Wrigley, E. A. (1973), *Identifying people in the past*, London: Arnold.

Wrigley, E. A.et al. (1997), *English population history from family reconstitution, 1580–1837*, Cambridge: Cambridge University Press.

INDEXES OF FAMILY HISTORIES

Barrow, Geoffrey B. (1977), *The genealogist's guide: An index to printed British pedigrees and family histories, 1950–1975*, London: Research Publishing Co.

Ferguson, Joan P. S. (compiler) (1986), *Scottish family histories*, Edinburgh: National Library of Scotland.

Grant, Francis J. (1908), *Index to genealogies, birthbriefs and funeral escutcheons recorded in the Lyon Office*, Edinburgh: Scottish Record Society.

Kaminkow, Marion J. (1967), *Genealogical manuscripts in British libraries: A descriptive guide*, Baltimore: Magna Charta Book Co.

Marshall, George W. [1903] (1998), *The genealogist's guide*, Baltimore: Clearfield, 1998.

Stuart, Margaret [1930] (1994), *Scottish family history: A guide to works of reference on the history and genealogy of Scottish families*, Baltimore: Genealogical Publishing Co. With an essay on how to write the history of a family, by Sir James Balfour Paul.

Thomson, T. R. (1980), *A catalogue of British family histories*, 3rd ed., London: Research Publishing Co.

Whitmore, J. B. (1953), *A genealogical guide: An index to British pedigrees in continuation of Marshall's Genealogist's guide, 1903*, London: Walford Bros.

IRISH FAMILY HISTORY

Fowler, Simon (2001), *Tracing Irish ancestors*, Kew: Public Record Office.

Griffith, Richard (1850–61), *General valuation of Ireland*, Dublin: Her Majesty's Stationery Office (available online).

Grenham, John (2006), *Tracing your Irish ancestors*, 3rd ed., Dublin: Gill and Macmillan.

Begley, Donal F. (ed.) (1984), *Handbook on Irish genealogy: How to trace your ancestors and relatives in Ireland*, 6th ed., Dublin: Heraldic Artists.

Index of Irish wills 1484–1858 (CD-ROM) (1999), Dublin: Eneclann.

JOURNALS

Ancestors: The family history magazine of the National Archives (2001), Kew: National Archives.

BBC, *Who do you think you are?* (2007), Bristol: Bristol Magazines.

Family history (1962), Canterbury: Institute of Heraldic and Genealogical Studies.

Family history monthly (1995), London: Diamond Publishing Group.

Family tree magazine (1984), Huntingdon: ABM Publishing.

Genealogical computing (1981), Salt Lake City: Ancestry Inc.

Genealogical periodical annual index (1962), Bowie, MD: Heritage Books.

Genealogists magazine (1925), London: Society of Genealogists.

Journal of family history: Studies in family, kinship and demography (1976), Thousand Oaks, CA: Sage.

Periodical source index (PERSI) (CD-ROM) (1987), Fort Wayne IA: Allen County Public Library. Subject index to genealogy and local history periodicals written in English and French (Canada) mainly since 1800, although some earlier material is included. Largest index of its type, with almost 5000 periodicals having been indexed. Also available to Ancestry. com subscribers.

Practical family history (1997), Huntingdon: ABM Publishing.

Raymond, Stuart A. (1991–4) (4 vols), *British genealogical periodicals: A bibliography of their contents*, Birmingham: Federation of Family History Societies; Exeter: S. A. and M. J. Raymond.

Scottish genealogist (1954), Edinburgh: Scottish Genealogy Society.

Your family tree (2003) Bath: Future.

LATIN

Gandy, Michael (1995), *Basic approach to Latin for family historians*, Birmingham: Federation of Family History Societies.

McLaughlin, Eve (1999), *Simple Latin for family historians*, 6th ed., Aylesbury: Varneys Press.

Martin, Charles Trice [1910] (1997), *The record interpreter: A collection of abbreviations, Latin words and names used in English historical manuscripts and records*, Baltimore: Clearfield.

Morris, Janet (1995), *A Latin glossary for family historians*, 2nd ed., Birmingham: Federation of Family History Societies.

Stuart, Denis (2006), *Latin for local and family historians*, Chichester: Phillimore.

NEWSPAPERS

Chapman, Colin R. (1993), *An introduction to using newspapers and periodicals*, Birmingham: Federation of Family History Societies.

Collins, Audrey (2001), *Using Colindale and other newspaper repositories*, Bury: Federation of Family History Societies.

Ferguson, Joan P. S. (1984), *Directory of Scottish newspapers*, Edinburgh: National Library of Scotland.

Glasgow Herald index 1906–84, available in the Mitchell Library, Glasgow.

McLaughlin, Eve (1994), *Family history from newspapers*, 2nd ed., Aylesbury: Varneys Press.

NONCONFORMISTS

Baptie, Diane (2000), *Records of baptisms, marriages and deaths in the Scottish secession churches (including lists of members)*, Aberdeen: Scottish Association of Family History Societies.

Breed, Geoffrey R. (2002), *My ancestors were Baptists: How can I find out more about them?*, 4th ed., London: Society of Genealogists.

Gandy, Michael (1993a), *Catholic missions and registers 1700–1880, volume 6: Scotland*, London: M. Gandy.

Gandy, Michael (1993b), *Catholic parishes in England, Wales and Scotland: An atlas*, London: M. Gandy.

Gandy, Michael (1996), *Catholic family history: A bibliography for Scotland*, London: M. Gandy.

Gandy, Michael (2001a), *Tracing Catholic ancestors*, Richmond: Public Record Office.

Gandy, Michael (2001b), *Tracing nonconformist ancestors*, Richmond: Public Record Office.

Joseph, Anthony (2005), *My ancestors were Jewish*, 4th ed., London: Society of Genealogists.

Leary, William (2005), *My ancestors were Methodists: How can I find out more about them?*, 4th ed., London: Society of Genealogists.

Logan, Roger (2000), *An introduction to Friendly Society records*, Bury: Federation of Family History Societies.

Milligan, Edward H. (1999), *My ancestors were Quakers: How can I find out more about them?*, 2nd rev. ed., London: Society of Genealogists.

Mordy, Isobel and Gandy, Michael (1996), *My ancestors were Jewish: How can I find out more about them?*, 2nd ed., London: Society of Genealogists.

Ruston, Alan (2001), *My ancestors were English Presbyterians or Unitarians: How can I find out more about them?*, 2nd ed., London: Society of Genealogists.

Steel, D. J. (ed.) (1972), *National Index of Parish Registers, volume 2: Sources for nonconformist genealogy and family history*, London: Society of Genealogists.

Steel, D. J. and Samuel, E. R. (1973), *National Index of Parish Registers, volume 3: Sources for Roman Catholic and Jewish genealogy and family history*, London: Society of Genealogists.

Wenzerul, Rosemary (2006), *Jewish ancestors?: A guide to Jewish genealogy in the United Kingdom*, London: Jewish Genealogical Society of Great Britain.

Wiggins, Ray (1999), *My ancestors were in the Salvation Army: How can I find out more about them?*, 2nd ed., London: Society of Genealogists.

OCCUPATIONS

Culling, Joyce (1999), *An introduction to occupations: A preliminary list*, 2nd ed., Birmingham: Federation of Family History Societies.

Raymond, Stuart A. (1996), *Occupational sources for genealogists: A bibliography*, 2nd ed., Birmingham: Federation of Family History Societies.

Torrance, D. Richard (1998), *Scottish trades, professions, vital records and directories: A selected bibliography*, Aberdeen: Scottish Association of Family History Societies.

Waters, Colin (2002), *A dictionary of old trades, titles and occupations*, new ed., Newbury: Countryside Books.

ARMED FORCES

Army

'Army list', 1740, 1754– (annual), London: War Office.

Dobson, David (1997a), *Scottish soldiers 1600-1800, part 1: registers of testaments*, St Andrews: David Dobson.

Dobson, David (1997b), *Scottish soldiers in Colonial America*, Baltimore: Clearfield.

Dobson, David (1997c), *Scottish soldiers in continental Europe, part. 1*, St Andrews: David Dobson.

Fowler, Simon (2006), *Tracing your army ancestors*, Barnsley: Pen and Sword Military.

Gibson, Jeremy and Dell, Alan (1991), *Tudor and Stuart muster rolls: A directory of holdings in the British Isles*, Birmingham: Federation of Family History Societies.

Gibson, Jeremy and Medlycott, Mervyn (2000), *Militia lists and musters 1757–1876: a directory of holdings in the British Isles*, 4th ed., Birmingham: Federation of Family History Societies.

Hamilton-Edwards, G. K. S. (1977), *In search of army ancestry*, London: Phillimore.

'Hart's annual army list', 1840–1916 (annual), London: J. Murray.

Spencer, William (2008), *Army records: A guide for family historians*, Kew: National Archives.

Spencer, William (1997), *Records of the militia and volunteer forces 1757–1945*, Richmond: Public Record Office.

Royal Air Force

'Air Force list', 1919–, London: HMSO.

Spencer, William (2008), *Air force records: A guide for family historians*, 2nd rev. ed., Kew: National Archives.

Royal Marines

Brooks, Richard and Little, Matthew (2008), *Tracing your Royal Marine ancestors: A guide for family historians*, Barnsley: Pen and Sword Military.

Divall, Ken (2008), *My ancestor was a Royal Marine*, London: Society of Genealogists.

Royal Navy

Cock, Randolph and Rodger, N. A. M. (eds) (2006), *Guide to the naval records in the National Archives of the UK*, London: Institute of Historical Research.

Marshall, John (1823–35) (12 vols), *Royal Naval biography*, London: various publishers.

'Navy list', 1814– (annual), London: HMSO.

'New navy list', 1839–55, London: various publishers.

O'Byrne, William R. (1849), *A naval biographical dictionary*, London: J. Murray.

Pappalardo, Bruno (2003), *Tracing your naval ancestors*, Kew: National Archives.

'Steel's navy list', 1782–1817 (annual), London: Steel.

CLERGY

Beckerlegge, Oliver A. (compiler) (1968), *United Methodist ministers and their circuits*, London: Epworth Press.

Bertie, David M. (2000), *Scottish Episcopal clergy, 1689–2000*, Edinburgh: T. and T. Clark.

'The Church College in Aberdeen: Free Church College 1843–1900, United Free Church 1900–1929, complete roll of alumni 1843–1929' (1936), Aberdeen: Aberdeen University Press.

Collins, G. N. M. (compiler) (1987), *Annals of the Free Church of Scotland 1900–1986: Continued from Ewing's Annals of the Free Church of Scotland: 1843–1900*, Edinburgh: Lindsay and Co.

Couper, William J. (1925), *The Reformed Presbyterian Church in Scotland, its congregations, ministers and students*, Edinburgh: United Free Church of Scotland Publication Dept. A Fasti of this Church 1743–1876.

'Crockford's clerical directory', (1858–), various publishers.

Ewing, William (1914) (2 vols), *Annals of the Free Church of Scotland 1843– 1900*, Edinburgh: T. and T. Clark.

Fasti Ecclesiae Scoticanae: The succession of Ministers in the Church of Scotland from 1560, (various dates) (9 vols), Edinburgh: Oliver and Boyd (Vols 1–8 available online).

Fasti Ecclesiae Scoticanae, volume 10: Ministers of the church from 1955–1975
(1981), Edinburgh: The Saint Andrew Press.

Forbes, F. and Anderson, W. J. (1966), 'Clergy lists of the Highland district,
1732–1828', *Innes Review*, 17, pp. 129–84.

Johnson, Christine (1989a), 'Scottish secular clergy, 1830–1878: The northern and eastern districts', *Innes Review*, 40, pp. 24–68.

Johnson, Christine (1989b), 'Scottish secular clergy, 1830–1878: The western
district, *Innes Review*, 40, pp. 106–52.

Lamb, John A. (1956), *The Fasti of the United Free Church of Scotland,
1900–1929*, Edinburgh: Oliver and Boyd.

Macgregor, W. M. (1930) *A souvenir of the Union in 1929: With an historical sketch of the United Free Church College, Glasgow . . . also a complete
alumnus roll from 1856–1929.* [Glasgow]: Trinity College Union.

MacKelvie, William (1873), *Annals and statistics of the United Presbyterian
Church*, Edinburgh: Oliphant and Co.

McNaughton, William D. (1993), *The Scottish Congregational ministry,
1794–1993*, Glasgow: Congregational Union of Scotland.

Small, Robert (1904) (2 vols), *History of the congregations of the United
Presbyterian Church from 1733–1900*, Edinburgh: David M. Small (available online).

Watt, D. E. R. and Murray, A. L. (eds) (2003), *Fasti ecclesiae Scoticanae medii
aevi ad annum 1638*, rev. ed., Edinburgh: Scottish Record Society.

LAWYERS

Grant, Sir Francis J. (1944), *The Faculty of Advocates in Scotland 1532–1943
with genealogical notes*, Edinburgh: Scottish Record Office.

Henderson, John Alexander (1912), *History of the Society of Advocates in
Aberdeen*, Aberdeen: New Spalding Club. Includes a list of members
1549-1911 with biographical notes (available online).

*History of the Society of Writers to her Majesty's Signet . . . with list of members
. . . from 1594 to 1890* (1890), Edinburgh: Society of Writers to her
Majesty's Signet (available online).

'Index juridicus: The Scottish law list 1846–1961', Edinburgh: A. and C. Black.

'Register of the Society of Writers to the Signet' (1983), Edinburgh: Clark,
Constable. Details of members from the fifteenth century to the 1980s.

MEDICAL AND RELATED PROFESSIONS

Amsden, Peter C. (2007), *The medical professions and their archives*, 2nd ed.,
Oban: ASAT Productions.

Bourne, Susan and Chicken, Andrew H. (1994), *Records of the medical profession: A practical guide for the family historian.* (n. p.): S. Bourne and
A. H. Chicken.

'Dentists register' 1879– (annual), London: various publishers.

'London & provincial medical directory' 1861–9, London: J. Churchill.

'Medical directory' 1845– (annual), London: Churchill Livingstone.

'Medical directory for Scotland 1852–1860', London: J. Churchill.

'Medical register' 1859– (annual), London: General Medical Council.

'Midwives roll' 1904–37 (annual), various publishers.

'Midwives roll' 1917– (annual), Edinburgh: Central Midwives Board for Scotland.

'Register of nurses' 1922–1968 (annual), London: General Nursing Council.

'Register of pharmaceutical chemists' 1869– (annual), London: Pharmaceutical Society of Great Britain.

'Register of chemists and druggists' 1869– (annual), London: Pharmaceutical Society of Great Britain.

Tough, Alister G. (1993) *Medical archives of Glasgow and Paisley: A guide to the Greater Glasgow Health Board Archive*, Glasgow: Wellcome Unit for the History of Medicine, University of Glasgow.

MERCHANTS AND TRADESMEN

Anderson, James R. (ed.) (1923–5), *The burgesses and guild brethren of Glasgow, 1573–1750*, Edinburgh: Scottish Record Society (available online).

Anderson, James R. (ed.) (1931–5), *The burgesses and guild brethren of Glasgow, 1751–1846*, Edinburgh: Scottish Record Society.

Armet, Helen (ed.) (1951), *Register of the burgesses of the Burgh of the Canongate: From 27th June, 1622 to 25th September 1733*, Edinburgh: Scottish Record Society (available online).

Beaton, Elizabeth A. and MacIntyre, Sheila W. (1990), *The burgesses of Inveraray, 1665–1963*, Edinburgh: Scottish Record Society.

Campbell, A. J. (1998), *Recorded indentures of apprenticeship*, Buckhaven: Fife Family History Society.

Dobson, David (2000), *The burgess rolls of Fife, 1700–1800, and St Andrews, 1700–1775*, Westminster, MD: Willow Bend Books.

Dobson, David (2002?), *Burgesses of Perth 1600–1699*, St Andrews: David Dobson.

Grant, Francis J. (ed.) (1906), *Register of apprentices of the city of Edinburgh, 1583–1666*, Edinburgh: Scottish Record Society (available online).

Harrison, John (1991), *Stirling burgess list*, Stirling: Central Scotland Family History Society.

Lindsay, Alistair and Kennedy, Jean B. (2002), *The burgesses and guild brethren of Ayr 1647–1846*, Drongan: Ayrshire Federation of Historical Societies.

McDonnell, Frances (1994a), *The burgess roll of Banff, 1549–1892*, St Andrews: F. McDonnell.

McDonnell, Frances (1994b), *The burgess roll of Elgin*, St Andrews: F. McDonnell.

McDonnell, Frances (1994c) (5 vols), *Register of merchant and trade burgesses of Aberdeen, 1600–1700*, St Andrews: F. McDonnell.

McDonnell, Frances (1994d), *Register of merchant and trade burgesses of Old Aberdeen, 1605–1725*, St Andrews: F. McDonnell.

McDonnell, Frances (1994e), *Register of merchant and trade burgesses of Old Aberdeen, 1726–1885*, St Andrews: F. McDonnell.

McDonnell, Frances (1998), *Roll of apprentices: Burgh of Aberdeen, 1622–1796*, St Andrews: Willow Bend Books.

Millar, A. H. (1887), *Roll of eminent burgesses of Dundee, 1513–1886*, Dundee: J. Leng and Co. (available online).

Munro, Alexander Macdonald (1890, 1906) (2 vols), *Register of Burgesses of the Burgh of Aberdeen, 1399-1631 (1631–1700)*, Aberdeen: New Spalding Club.

Roberts, Fergus (compiler) (1937), *Roll of Dumbarton burgesses and guild-brethren, 1600–1846: With a continuation thereof to the present day*, Edinburgh: Scottish Record Society.

Roll of guild burgesses of the royal burgh of Aberdeen, 1399–1631 (1890), Aberdeen: [s.n.].

Torrance, D. Richard (1997), *Kirkcudbright burgesses 1576 to 1975*, Edinburgh: D. R. Torrance.

Watson, Charles B. Boog (ed.) (1929), *Register of Edinburgh apprentices, 1666–1700*, Edinburgh: Scottish Record Society.

Watson, Charles B. Boog (ed.) (1929), *Register of Edinburgh apprentices, 1701–1755*, Edinburgh: Scottish Record Society.

Watson, Charles B. Boog (ed.) (1926–9), *Roll of Edinburgh burgesses and guild-brethren, 1406–1700*, Edinburgh: Scottish Record Society.

Watson, Charles B. Boog (ed.) (1929–30), *Roll of Edinburgh burgesses and guild-brethren, 1701–1760*, Edinburgh: Scottish Record Society.

Watson, Charles B. Boog (ed.) (1933), *Roll of Edinburgh burgesses and guild-brethren, 1761–1841*, Edinburgh: Scottish Record Society.

Wood, Marguerite (ed.) (1963), *Register of Edinburgh apprentices, 1756–1800*, Edinburgh: Scottish Record Society.

TEACHERS

Aberdeen Church of Scotland Training College (1896), *The Church of Scotland Training College in Aberdeen: Records of the classes from 1874–75 to 1894–95*, Aberdeen: Adelphi.

Aberdeen Church of Scotland Training College (1907), *The Church of Scotland Training College in Aberdeen: Records of the classes from 1895–96 to 1905–07*, Aberdeen: Albany Press.

Cowper, A. S. (ed.) (1997), *SSPCK schoolmasters, 1709–1872*, Edinburgh: Scottish Record Society.

Dobson, David (1998), *Scottish school masters of the seventeenth century, part 1*, Westminster, MD: Heritage Books.

OTHER OCCUPATIONS

British railways pre-grouping atlas and gazetteer (1997), 5th ed., Shepperton: Ian Allan.

Dobson, David. Many titles on Scottish seafarers. Check library catalogues.

Dobson, David (199–?), *Scottish goldsmiths, 1600–1800*, St Andrews: David Dobson.

Edwards, Cliff (2001), *Railway records: A guide to sources*, Richmond: Public Record Office.

Fowler, Simon (2003), *Researching brewery and publican ancestors*, Bury: Federation of Family History Societies.

Gibson, Jeremy and Hunter, Judith (1997), *Victuallers' licences: Records for family and local historians*, 2nd ed., Birmingham: Federation of Family History Societies.

Hogg, Peter L. (1997), *Using merchant ship records for family historians*, Birmingham: Federation of Family History Societies.

Hurley, Beryl (ed.) (1991–4) (3 vols), *The book of trades, or, Library of useful arts*, Devizes: Wiltshire Family History Society. Reproduced from editions of 1811 and 1818.

Loverseed, D. E. (1994), *Gasworker ancestors: How to find out more about them: a guide to genealogical sources for the British gas industry*, Stockport: DCS.

Richards, Tom (2002), *Was your grandfather a railwayman?: A directory of records*, 4th ed., Bury: Federation of Family History Societies. Covers UK and other countries.

Shearman, Antony (2000), *My ancestor was a policeman: How can I find out more about him?*, London: Society of Genealogists.

Tonks, David (2003), *My ancestor was a coalminer*, London: Society of Genealogists.

Torrance, D. Richard (1998), *Scottish trades, professions, vital records and directories: A selected bibliography*, Aberdeen: Scottish Association of Family History Societies.

Waters, Colin (2002), *A dictionary of old trades, titles and occupations*, new ed., Newbury: Countryside Books.

Watts, Christopher T. and Michael J. (2002), *My ancestor was a merchant seaman: How can I find out more about him?*, 2nd ed., London: Society of Genealogists.

Whyte, Donald (1996), *Scottish clock and watch makers, 1453–1900*, Edinburgh: Scottish Genealogy Society.

Whyte, Donald (2001a), *Clock and watchmakers of the Scottish Borders, 1556–1990*, Kirkliston: D. Whyte.

Whyte, Donald (2001b), *Clock and watchmakers of the Scottish Highlands and islands, 1780–1900: includes Moray and Nairn*, [n. p.]: Highland Family History Society.

OTHER SPECIFIC SOURCES

Amsden, Peter C. (1999), *Basic approach to making contact with relatives*, Bury: Federation of Family History Societies.

Birthlink Adoption Counselling Centre at Family Care (1997), *Search guide for adopted people in Scotland*, London: Stationery Office.

Chapman, Colin R. (1996), *Marriage laws, rites, records and customs: Was your ancestor really married?*, Dursley: Lochin Publishing.

Decennial indexes to the services of heirs in Scotland 1700–1859, Edinburgh: HMSO.

Escott, Anne (1986), *Census returns and old parochial registers on microfilm: A directory of public library holdings in the West of Scotland*, rev. ed., Glasgow: Glasgow District Libraries.

Floate, Sharon Sillers (1999), *My ancestors were Gypsies*, London: Society of Genealogists.

Gibbens, Lilian (1994), *An introduction to church registers*, Birmingham: Federation of Family History Societies.

Gibson, Jeremy and Hampson, Elizabeth (2000), *Specialist indexes for family historians*, 2nd ed., Bury: Federation of Family History Societies.

Gibson, Jeremy, Hampson, Elizabeth and Raymond, Stuart (2007), *Marriage indexes for family historians*, 9th ed., Bury: The Family History Partnership.

Gibson, Jeremy and Rogers, Colin (1996), *Electoral registers since 1832; and burgess rolls*, 2nd ed., Birmingham: Federation of Family History Societies.

Gibson, Jeremy and Rogers, Colin (2008), *Poll books 1696–1872: a directory to holdings in Great Britain*, 4th ed., Bury: The Family History Partnership.

Inquisitionum ad Capellam Domini Regis retornatarum (1811–1816) (3 vols), [London]. Summary of retours before 1700.

Lewis, Pat (1999), *My ancestor was a Freemason*, London: Society of Genealogists.

Litton, Pauline with Chapman, Colin (1996), *Basic facts about using marriage records for family historians*, Birmingham: Federation of Family History Societies.

Litton, Pauline (1996), *Using baptism records for family historians*, Birmingham: Federation of Family History Societies.

McLaughlin, Eve (1985), *Interviewing elderly relatives*, 2nd ed., Plymouth: Federation of Family History Societies.

The parishes, registers and registrars of Scotland (1993), [Aberdeen]: Scottish Association of Family History Societies (1997 reprint).

Probert, Eric D. (1994), *Company and business records for family historians*, Birmingham: Federation of Family History Societies.

Raymond, Stuart A. (2001), *Using libraries: Workshops for family historians*, Bury: Federation of Family History Societies.

Retours of services of heirs, covering the period 1544–1699 (CD-ROM), Edinburgh: Scottish Genealogy Society.

Services of heirs in Scotland, covering the period 1700–1859 (CD-ROM), Edinburgh: Scottish Genealogy Society.

Shaw, Gareth and Tipper, Allison (1997), *British directories: A bibliography and guide to directories published in England and Wales, 1850–1950; and Scotland, 1773–1950*, 2nd ed., New York: Mansell.

Sinclair, Cecil (2000), *Jock Tamson's bairns: A history of the records of the General Register Office for Scotland*, Edinburgh: General Register Office for Scotland.

Swinnerton, Iain (1995), *Basic facts about sources for family history in the home*, Birmingham: Federation of Family History Societies.

Swinnerton, Iain (2001), *Identifying your World War I soldier from badges and photographs*, Bury: Federation of Family History Societies.

Timperley, Loretta R. (1976), *A directory of landownership in Scotland, c.1770*, Edinburgh: Scottish Record Society.

Using birth, marriage and death records (2000), Richmond: Public Record Office.

PEERAGE AND LANDED GENTRY

Burke's family index (1976), London: Burke's Peerage.

Burke's peerage, baronetage and knightage (2003) (3 vols), 107th ed., Stokesley: Burke's Peerage and Gentry (available online).

Burke's landed gentry of Great Britain (2001–5) (4 vols), 19th ed., Stokesley: Burke's Peerage and Gentry (available online).

Debrett's peerage and baronetage (2008), 147th ed., Richmond: Debrett's.

Paul, Sir James Balfour (1904–1914) (9 vols), *The Scots peerage*, Edinburgh: D. Douglas.

CD-ROM version, Edinburgh: Scottish Genealogy Society.

PHOTOGRAPHS

Linkman, A. (1991), *Caring for your family photographs at home*, Manchester: Documentary Photography Archive.

Oliver, George (1989), *Photographs and local history*, London: Batsford.

Pols, Robert (1999), *Looking at old photographs: Their dating and interpretation*, Newbury: Countryside Books.

Pols, Robert (2002), *Family photographs, 1860–1945*, Richmond: Public Record Office.

Pols, Robert (2005), *Dating nineteenth century photographs*, Bury: Federation of Family History Societies.

Shrimpton, Jayne (2008), *Family photographs and how to date them*, Newbury: Countryside Books.

Steel, D. J. and Taylor, L. (eds) (1984), *Family history in focus*, Guildford: Lutterworth Press.

RECORDING AND WRITING YOUR FAMILY HISTORY

Bannister, Shala Mills (1994), *Family treasures: Videotaping your family history: A guide for preserving your family's living history as an heirloom for future generations*, Baltimore: Genealogical Publishing Co.

Best, Laura (2005), *Scrapbooking your family history*, New York: Sterling Publishing.

Calder, A. and Lockwood, V. (1993), *Shooting video history: A video workshop on video recording for family and community historians, with accompanying notes*, Milton Keynes: The Open University.

Carmack, Sharon DeBartolo (2008), *You can write your family history*, Baltimore: Genealogical Publishing Co.

Cass, Deborah (2004), *Writing your family history: A practical guide*, Ramsbury: Crowood.

Chapman, Philip J. (2000), *Basic approach to illuminating your family history with picture postcards*, Bury: Federation of Family History Societies.

Fitzhugh, Terrick V. H. and Fitzhugh, Henry (2005), *How to write your family history*, rev. ed., Yeovil: Marston House.

Gale, Thornton and Gale, Marty (2007), *Getting started on your genealogy website*, Mercer Island, WA: www.genealogyhosting.com.

Huberman, Rob and Huberman, Laura (2003), *How to create a video family history: The complete guide to interviewing and taping your family's stories and memories*, Margate, NJ: ComteQ Press.

Kita, Suzanne and Kinghorn, Harriet R. (2002), *Videotape your memoirs: The perfect way to preserve your family's history*, Sanger, CA: Quill Driver Books.

Lynskey, Marie (1996), *Family trees: A manual for their design, layout and display*, Chichester: Phillimore.

McClure, Rhonda R. (2004), *Digitizing your family history: Easy methods for preserving your heirloom documents, photos, home movies and more in a digital format*, Cincinnati: Family Tree Books.

McLaughlin, Eve (1988), *Laying out a pedigree*, Birmingham: Federation of Family History Societies.

Palgrave-Moore, Patrick (1994), *How to record your family tree*, 6th ed., Norwich: Elvery Dowers Publications.

Phillimore, W. P. W. [1888?] (1972), *How to write the history of a family*, 2nd ed., Detroit: Gale Research Co.

Swinnerton, Iain (1999), *Basic approach to keeping your family records*, 2nd ed., Birmingham: Federation of Family History Societies.

Titford, John (2003), *Writing up your family history: A do-it-yourself guide*, 2nd ed., Newbury: Countryside Books.

Trubshaw, Bob (2005), *How to write and publish local and family history successfully: Books, booklets, magazines, CD-ROMs and web sites*, Loughborough: Heart of Albion.

STUDY OF GENEALOGY

Sayers, S. (1984), 'The psychological significance of genealogy', in Paul Smith (ed.), *Perspectives on contemporary legend*, Sheffield: Centre for English Cultural Tradition and Language, University of Sheffield.

Wagner, Sir Anthony (1961), *English ancestry*, London: Oxford University Press.

Wagner, Sir Anthony (1975), *Pedigree and progress*, London: Phillimore.

Wagner, Sir Anthony (1983), *English genealogy*, 3rd ed., Chichester: Phillimore.

SURNAMES

Bardsley, Alan (2003), *First name variants*, 3rd ed., Birmingham: Federation of Family History Societies.

Black, George F. [1946] (1996), *The surnames of Scotland: Their origin, meaning and history*, Edinburgh: Birlinn.

Donaldson, Gordon (1981), *Surnames and ancestry in Scotland*, [Scotland: G. Donaldson].

Dorward, David (2003), *Scottish surnames*, new ed., Edinburgh: Mercat.

Hanks, Patrick and Hodges, Flavia (2002), *A concise dictionary of surnames*, Oxford: Oxford University Press.

McKinley, Richard (1990), *A history of British surnames*, London: Longman.

Reaney, P. H. (1979), *A dictionary of British surnames*, 2nd ed., London: Routledge and Kegan Paul.

Rogers, Colin (1995), *The surname detective*, Manchester: Manchester University Press.

Whyte, Donald (2000), *Scottish surnames*, 2nd ed., Edinburgh: Birlinn.

WILLS

Camp, A. J. (1974), *Wills and their whereabouts*, 4th ed., Canterbury: Phillimore.

Gibson, Jeremy (2002), *Probate jurisdictions: Where to look for wills*, 5th ed., Bury: Federation of Family History Societies.

Taylor, Nigel and Grannum, Karen (2009), *Wills and probate records: A guide for family historians*, Kew: National Archives.

Vicars, Sir Arthur (ed.) (1897), *Index to the Prerogative Wills of Ireland, 1536–1810*, Dublin: E. Ponsonby.

INDEX